Patricia D. Nanoff, DMin

Rising from the Dead
Stories of Women's Spiritual Journeys to Sobriety

Pre-publication
REVIEWS,
COMMENTARIES,
EVALUATIONS . . .

"Recovering people know well that stories are the vehicles of our most powerful understandings of God. Now Patricia Nanoff has demonstrated the healing power of 'feminist listening' in this remarkable journey with a group who have been vastly misunderstood and underrepresented in recovery literature: alcoholic women in long-term sobriety. Repeatedly etched throughout these women's stories are the themes of new life, new community, and new visions of the sacred, and Nanoff weaves these themes into an effective demonstration of narrative counseling. Particularly compelling is her understanding of healing from shame as a deeply incarnational process grounded in spiritual community. This book is a splendid resource for both therapists and religious leaders—and it is a joyful celebration of true resurrection in recovering women."

James B. Nelson, PhD
Professor Emeritus of Christian Ethics,
United Theological Seminary
of the Twin Cities; Author, *Thirst:
God and the Alcoholic Experience*

More pre-publication
REVIEWS, COMMENTARIES, EVALUATIONS . . .

"This book is highly effective in revealing the power of redemption and the joy of healing. The women's stories are compelling as well as empowering to the reader. This is a must-read for substance abuse practitioners, whether they are of the twelve-step tradition or as myself, of the harm-reduction school; pastoral counselors will find much of value here. Nanoff writes with conviction yet not dogmatically from the perspective of a feminist Christian theologian and clinical social worker as she takes us into the world of women who have found a 'pathway from hell to redemption.' Nanoff, through her skillful editing of interviews with women in recovery, maps the territory of their journeys so that others might follow the same path and find hope even in the most depressing of circumstances. Women battling the throes of addiction willing to embark on a spiritual journey will find many gems in this delightful volume on spiritual growth and recovery. Social work educators will find much of interest here for use in their teaching. Pastors will certainly want to keep copies on hand to share with members of the congregation dealing with issues related to alcoholism and drug use. Because the book is relevant to women's issues, counselors in women's shelters might well keep a supply on hand to share with residents who so often have a history of alcohol problems."

Katherine van Wormer, MSSW, PhD
Professor of Social Work,
University of Northern Iowa;
Co-author, *Addiction Treatment:*
A Strengths Perspective

The Haworth Pastoral Press Press®
An Imprint of The Haworth Press, Inc.
New York

Rising from the Dead
Stories of Women's Spiritual Journeys to Sobriety

THE HAWORTH PASTORAL PRESS®
Religion and Mental Health
Harold G. Koenig, MD
Senior Editor

Pastoral Care for Post-Traumatic Stress Disorder: Healing the Shattered Soul by Daléne Fuller Rogers

Integrating Spirit and Psyche: Using Women's Narratives in Psychotherapy by Mary Pat Henehan

Chronic Pain: Biomedical and Spiritual Approaches by Harold G. Koenig

Spirituality in Pastoral Counseling and the Community Helping Professions by Charles Topper

Parish Nursing: A Handbook for the New Millennium edited by Sybil D. Smith

Mental Illness and Psychiatric Treatment: A Guide for Pastoral Counselors by Gregory B. Collins and Thomas Culbertson

The Power of Spirituality in Therapy: Integrating Spiritual and Religious Beliefs in Mental Health Practice by Peter A. Kahle and John M. Robbins

Bereavement Counseling: Pastoral Care for Complicated Grieving by Junietta Baker McCall

Biblical Stories for Psychotherapy and Counseling: A Sourcebook by Matthew B. Schwartz and Kalman J. Kaplan

A Christian Approach to Overcoming Disability: A Doctor's Story by Elaine Leong Eng

Faith, Medicine, and Science: A Festschrift in Honor of Dr. David B. Larson edited by Jeff Levin and Harold G. Koenig

Encyclopedia of Ageism by Erdman Palmore, Laurence Branch, and Diana Harris

Dealing with the Psychological and Spiritual Aspects of Menopause: Finding Hope in the Midlife by Dana E. King, Melissa H. Hunter, and Jerri R. Harris

Spirituality and Mental Health: Clinical Applications by Gary W. Hartz

Dying Declarations: Notes from a Hospice Volunteer by David B. Resnik

Maltreatment of Patients in Nursing Homes: There Is No Safe Place by Diana K. Harris and Michael L. Benson

Is There a God in Health Care? Toward a New Spirituality of Medicine by William F. Haynes and Geffrey B. Kelly

Guide to Ministering to Alzheimer's Patients and Their Families by Patricia A. Otwell

The Unwanted Gift of Grief: A Ministry Approach by Tim P. VanDuivendyk

The Treatment of Bipolar Disorder in Pastoral Counseling: Community and Silence by David Welton

Rising from the Dead: Stories of Women's Spiritual Journeys to Sobriety by Patricia D. Nanoff

Rising from the Dead
Stories of Women's Spiritual Journeys to Sobriety

Patricia D. Nanoff, DMin, LICSW

The Haworth Pastoral Press Press®
An Imprint of The Haworth Press, Inc.
New York

For more information on this book or to order, visit
http://www.haworthpress.com/store/product.asp?sku=5800

or call 1-800-HAWORTH (800-429-6784) in the United States and Canada
or (607) 722-5857 outside the United States and Canada

or contact orders@HaworthPress.com

Published by

The Haworth Pastoral Press®, an imprint of The Haworth Press, Inc., 10 Alice Street, Binghamton,
NY 13904-1580.

PUBLISHER'S NOTE
The development, preparation, and publication of this work has been undertaken with great care.
However, the Publisher, employees, editors, and agents of The Haworth Press are not responsible
for any errors contained herein or for consequences that may ensue from use of materials or
information contained in this work. The Haworth Press is committed to the dissemination of ideas
and information according to the highest standards of intellectual freedom and the free exchange of
ideas. Statements made and opinions expressed in this publication do not necessarily reflect the
views of the Publisher, Directors, management, or staff of The Haworth Press, Inc., or an
endorsement by them.

Cover design by Kerry E. Mack.

The Twelve Steps and Twelve Traditions and a brief excerpt from the book, *Alcoholics Anonymous*
are reprinted with permission of Alcoholics Anonymous World Services, Inc. (AAWS). Permission
to reprint a brief excerpt from the book, *Alcoholics Anonymous* the Twelve Steps and Twelve Traditions does not mean that AAWS has reviewed or approved the contents of this publication, or that
AAWS necessarily agrees with the views expressed herein. AA is a program of recovery from alcoholism *only*—use of the Twelve Steps and Twelve Traditions in connection with programs and
activities which are patterned after AA, but which address other problems, or in any other non-AA
context, does not imply otherwise.

Lyrics from the "Song of the Body of Christ" by David Haas. Copyright © 1989 by GIA Publications, Inc., 7404 S. Mason Ave., Chicago, IL 60638. www.giamusic.com 800.422.1358 All rights
reserved. Used by permission.

Quoted material in Chapter 8 from Roberta Bondi, *Memories of God: Theoretical Reflections on a
Life*. Abingdon Press, 1995, p. 201. Used by permission.

Library of Congress Cataloging-in-Publication Data

Nanoff, Patricia D.
　　Rising from the dead : stories of women's spiritual journeys to sobriety / Patricia D. Nanoff.
　　　　p. cm.
　　Includes bibliographical references and index.
　　ISBN: 978-0-7890-3173-0 (case : alk. paper)
　　ISBN: 978-0-7890-3174-7 (soft : alk. paper)
　　1. Alcoholism—Religious aspects—Christianity. 2. Women alcoholics—Rehabilitation—United
States. 3. Women alcoholics—United States—Biography. I. Title.

BV4596.A48N36 2007
248.8'6292082—dc22
　　　　　　　　　　　　　　　　　　　　　　　　　　　　　　　　　　2006036252

For my mother Jeanne Villas Dorsey

ABOUT THE AUTHOR

Patricia Dorsey Nanoff, DMin, LICSW, is Associate Professor at the College of St. Catherine in Minneapolis, Minnesota, where she teaches in the areas of theology and applied medical ethics. Prior to her teaching career, she worked as a consultant and trainer in the areas of chemical dependency and family systems, and as a therapist in private practice. She has trained both nationally and internationally in the areas of alcoholism recovery, narrative construction, and spirituality of recovery.

He descended into hell; the third day he rose again from the dead.

Apostles' Creed

We come to tell our story,
We come to break the bread,
We come to know our rising from the dead.

David Haas

Religion is for people who are afraid of hell.
Spirituality is for people who have been there.

Overheard at an AA meeting

CONTENTS

Acknowledgments

As I consider all of the people who have assisted with this project I find that I have a new understanding of and appreciation for the communion of saints! I offer thanks to Marilaurice Hemlock for her gentle guidance and amazing liturgical sensibilities. I offer thanks to Robin Lukes for allowing me to think out loud in her presence as a way to understand the stories that had come to me. I offer thanks to Sr. Marcie Anibas FSPA, and to the women of WomanWell whose deep and abiding stories helped shape my reflection on the stories that follow. Many friends and colleagues read all or parts of this project and gave thoughtful comment and criticism including Mary Kaye Medinger and Margaret Post. Very critical to the success of this project were the efforts of PH, CM, and MJD who assisted in identifying the great elder storytellers whose life narratives are featured. I offer thanks for Jeanne McPhee's angelic inspiration and to my husband Carl for encouraging me to take the space to think and write and who is my most cherished thinking partner! Finally, I offer humble thanks to the women elders in Alcoholics Anonymous, whose life stories were given so generously and whose spirits, I believe, represent the light of God's love in the world.

PART I:
WE COME TO TELL OUR STORY

Chapter 1

A Conversation in Ordinary Time

On a hot and humid Sunday, the Gospel reading focused on wheat and chaff. I had been forewarned about the Gospel because the Lutheran church near my home had posted the sermon title "Dealing with Weeds." The guest homilist at our small Catholic church read from the text for the thirteenth Sunday in ordinary time, Matthew 13:23-44. Like our Lutheran neighbors, we were having a go at it, including the metaphor of weeds. At the end of the homily the community was invited to step to microphones located around the worship space and offer a comment or two. As members fanned themselves with bulletins and worship aids and mopped brows wet from the oppressive humidity, a few folks stood and made comments. Most talked about the recent rains and their effects on gardens. One woman talked about a volunteer experience where she found herself planting native wildflowers and vegetation a scant week after pulling similar plants from her own garden. Finally, an active member of our community—a woman sober for twenty-four years—stepped to the microphone and offered a bit of translation. Her comments went something like this: "I am a member of Alcoholics Anonymous. We refer to our 'chaff' or 'weeds' as character defects. In the sixth step of Alcoholics Anonymous we become ready to have God remove these defects of character. And in the seventh step we humbly ask God to remove our shortcomings. I have found in my years of sobriety that it is best to leave to God what is removed and what is left to bloom." "Ah," said the collective community and we moved on to the prayers of the faithful. . . .

THE POWER OF STORIES

This book is about alcoholic women. It documents the spiritual life stories of women who became sober at a time when being an alcoholic woman placed one so far beyond the pale that she was considered to be literally beyond redemption. The women who volunteered their stories for this book did so in the hope that women who still suf-

fer might find some solace in their shared stories, and in the hope that
pastors, pastoral counselors, and chaplains in the Christian community might learn something about walking the territory of fallenness
so familiar to these women. Among us are anonymous women who
entered the tunnel that leads to hell and yet found their way back.
They are often seen as the weeds and chaff of our communities; however, their stories reveal the powerful reconciling presence of God.
This book documents their stories and their unique way of telling stories. There is an unnecessary disconnect between the redemption stories found in the recovering community and the faith communities
where many of the dramas play out. This is a love story. I found great
integrity and strength in these wonderful elders; theirs is a generosity
of spirit that is compelling. The path they have traveled and the spirituality they practice is not for everyone—this book is not an apology
for Alcoholics Anonymous. The goal of this book is to map the territory between the individual shattered life and the Christian faith communities where reconciliation might take place, between the vibrant
spirituality of the twelve steps and helping professionals who have
not yet learned to speak that language.

This book came about, in part, because of my own story. My story
is an ordinary one. I grew up in an alcoholic family and I began my
own personal spiritual journey of reconciliation in the spring of 1973.
This experience has been a blessing beyond words and is noteworthy
because telling one's own story is a departure from commonly held
"best practices" for pastoral care, counseling, and health care. Current expectations require the helping professional to submerge the
personal in order to hear the story being offered, yet the field of alcoholism has long practiced counseling strategies that require something quite different, that is, that the story of the counselor is not only
relevant but necessary to the therapeutic relationship. My own story
matters, counts, when engaging in relationship with those I counsel.

A belief in the power and relevance of one's own story can be
viewed as one kind of feminist theological practice. In fact, theologians practicing womanist theology highlight the power and deep significance of personal story. Theologian Delores S. Williams begins
her powerful book *Sisters in the Wilderness: The Challenge of
Womanist God-Talk* by inviting theologians to tell some part of their
own stories as one way of locating their theological work.[1] Williams
defines womanist theology as a kind of "prophetic voice" theology

that is concerned with justice issues within the African-American community.[2] For Williams and others practicing feminist and womanist theology, one's own story and the stories of others provide a context or framework for more abstract principles such as salvation and reconciliation—indeed, womanist theology reminds us that the most powerful theological principles are expressed within the context of story. Stories are the carriers, the containers for our most sacred and powerful understandings of the self and of God.

How is this relevant to the discussion at hand? For alcoholic women, context is everything. The matrix of shame and remorse that binds the suffering alcoholic is in fact the very matrix that can provide relief, reconciliation, and redemption. The situations and choices that have caused harm, made her feel ashamed and diminished become the vehicle for God's grace and reconciling action. The very choices that lead to an intrapsychic break become the means for reconnection, and ultimately, the vehicle through which others are healed and reconciled as well. The experience of active alcoholism is exactly like descending into hell. The women who suffer with addiction are almost never living life in ordinary time—their pain and suffering moves them to another more terrifying and extraordinary place. Only entry into God's own sacred space can reclaim them. This book is a guide for the helping professional who wants to understand that particular pathway from hell to redemption.

I will focus exclusively on the stories of recovering women because their stories tend not to be told. Women's stories are underrepresented in the literature on addiction therapy and their experience is often misunderstood or misrepresented. While conducting the initial research for this project it became painfully clear that little is written about women with long-term sobriety and they face psychological discrimination when they reveal their recovery in public spaces. It is not necessary to detail what the greater society thinks of alcoholic women. To be an alcoholic woman is to stand accused by society in the most shameful way. This attitude is pervasive and often toxic for women as they seek treatment and recovery, yet the stories offered by the women I interviewed trace a path through such treacherous territory.

Who are the storytellers? The women whose stories are represented here were identified through my contacts within the community of Alcoholics Anonymous and by word of mouth. Those who participated had achieved lengths of sobriety ranging from twenty-five to fifty-three years. They originated from various regions of the United States including Minnesota, Missouri, Oklahoma, Texas, and Pennsylvania. Their ages ranged from forty-six to ninety years old. All of the interviews were conducted in person. The participants were asked to tell their life stories following a formula frequently used in Alcoholics Anonymous meetings worldwide: tell how it was, what happened, and how it is now.[3] I used this familiar formula as a means of understanding and documenting what these women with long-term sobriety "know" and how they have come to know it. Amazingly, when approached none of the participants asked me for identification or any proof of professional credentials. Rather, they identified my credibility and trustworthiness via my connection to those they knew in the recovery community. Any expertise I might have as a clinical social worker or as a theologian was seen, at best, as secondary to my knowledge and understanding of the language and practice of recovery. Had I not been a fluent speaker of the recovery language these particular stories would not have been offered. During the interviews I became aware of the "hidden" quality of the stories; theirs is a powerful presence that operates below radar.

A deep and uncharted ocean of stories is held by the community of recovering alcoholics. These stories are transmitted by word of mouth and, although audiotapes are circulated that feature well-known speakers at conventions, stories such as the ones contained here are not part of any documented record. These stories live by breath alone, transmitted through the sighs and silences at AA meetings. I decided to record these stories as a way of capturing a small bit of the fire and light that they provide and I am painfully aware that in documenting them something essential has been lost. In my time with the long-sober women of AA I learned that in hearing the spoken stories and the silences between them, the real spirit of the story is revealed. These stories offer a dynamic model of life-reclamation that is of significance for pastoral ministers in their work with women who suffer from alcoholism.

I want to acknowledge also that this book relies a great deal on the language of twelve-step recovery. If this language is new to you, some of the references could be a bit puzzling. Some basic details may be helpful. AA offers the following self-description:

We are not an organization in the conventional sense of the word. There are no fees or dues whatsoever. The only requirement for membership is an honest desire to stop drinking. We are not allied with any particular faith, sect or denomination, nor do we oppose anyone. We simply wish to be helpful to those who are afflicted.[4]

Members of AA follow a program of recovery based on the twelve steps and twelve traditions that are detailed in the foundational book *Alcoholics Anonymous,* referred to by members as the "Big Book" and in the companion book *Twelve Steps and Twelve Traditions,* referred to by members as the "twelve-by-twelve."[5]

FROM ORDINARY TO EXTRAORDINARY

The stories documented in the pages that follow offer one model—to call on language suggested by Rebecca Chopp—of storycrafting as salvage, as saving work.[6] The process of storycrafting discussed in the chapters that follow provides an amazing map that has great value for those practicing pastoral care, counseling, and for anyone working to strengthen a community of faith. The women who agreed to tell their stories for this book are living out their lives in the place where ordinary time and sacred time meet. This is part of what makes their stories so compelling. Their lives embody one type of sacred reality that lives within ordinary time; theirs is the extraordinary revealed within the ordinary. While I expected to hear good and entertaining stories when I began research for this book, I was unprepared for the thunderous, spirit-filled nature of these narratives. The very fact that these lives are considered by their owners to be "commonplace" has changed my understanding of the activity of God's spirit in the world.

What is the difference between ordinary time and sacred time as experienced by the women of this study? How does time become transformed? We live much of our lives in ordinary time. This means that our lives take on a shape that is familiar and routine. We may experience highs and lows, but they are mundane and in many ways predictable. These ordinary times are interrupted by birthdays and holidays, but even the interruptions have a familiar form and function in our lives. However, some ordinary experiences interrupt ordinary time in fresh and new ways, transforming ordinary time into extraordinary time. We know intuitively that birth is an ordinary occurrence; in the time it took me to write this sentence many new souls were welcomed by families. These events are noteworthy because they are both ordinary and extraordinary—we could say that they are "ordinary" in the abstract and "extraordinary" in the particular. If it is my child that is born the experience is anything but ordinary! The same dynamic is operating when someone dies; death is ordinary until it is the death of someone I know and love.

The experience of transformed time is of particular interest when considering alcoholism and its consequences for those who love the alcoholic. In the alcoholic family, ordinary times become twisted into extraordinarily difficult times and family members find themselves yearning for the peace of the mundane; however, this is not the only instance where ordinary time becomes transformed. As I have begun to share what I learned while researching this book, I have been reminded how true this experience rings for people living with other life-changing situations and events. Death of a loved one, divorce, protracted or terminal illness, all hold the capacity to shift us from ordinary to extraordinary time. This is one of the gifts of the stories given for this book—a grace is revealed when we navigate this territory.

In the chapters that follow we will trace the path from ordinary to extraordinary, and in doing so perhaps capture some small sense of the breath of God moving within the ordinary and transforming it into the sacred extraordinary. The shape of this book is meant to mirror the process encountered in the Christian liturgical year with a special focus on Lent, the time between Ash Wednesday and Pentecost. We will follow the move from ordinary time to sacred time, mirroring the liturgical journey that is so integral to Christian life and tradition. We began with a brief conversation in ordinary time. The chapters that follow consider life narratives within the liturgical framework described in the lyrics from "Song of the Body of Christ"

> We come to tell our story.
> We come to break the bread.
> We come to know our rising from the dead.[7]

In Chapter 1, the women tell their stories as they would in AA meetings and no interpreting theory is brought to bear on the narratives as they have been offered. In Chapters 2 and 3, the same narratives are broken open and the inner workings are considered within the context of more secular models of alcoholism treatment. In Chapters 4 through 8, the narratives are considered in relationship to theological categories and models. Chapter 9 discusses barriers specific to helping professionals and pastoral counselors. Chapter 10 considers specific suggestions for the use of story in pastoral ministry and specific tools and strategies for pastoral counseling are detailed. In this way then, liturgical time serves as the container or frame for the examination of the process of story crafting as the genesis of one kind of sacramental encounter.

Chapter 2

Entering Sacred Space

STORYCRAFTING

What is the purpose of narrative construction in the recovery process? Plainly spoken, what is story for? NH posed this question to me when she agreed to tell me her story. It was her concern that her story have some utility, that it be *for* someone, that there be a person who needs to hear what she has to say. During a telephone conversation she explained to me that when she tells her story at AA meetings she is certain that God will lead her to say whatever is needed for the person who needs to hear her story. Before she would agree to tell her story for this book she needed to think about whether there might be someone who needed to hear something from God, and she believed firmly that this "something" would be expressed within her life experiences. This criterion had to be satisfied before NH agreed to speak to me; without it her story would be meaningless, or worse, an exercise in pure ego. I note this detail because it is essential to the approach of storytelling found in AA. And although this formula for narrative construction is not stated explicitly in AA literature, except in one or two places, it is so much a part of the expectations of those in AA that it was assumed by all who participated. Consider the uniqueness of this approach to storytelling: *God will use my story to communicate to you. My story participates in the active reconciling grace of God in the world.*

Story is the central element of the fellowship of Alcoholics Anonymous. The sociological impact of AA and related movements is undeniable and well documented.[1] Members of AA operate within a subculture with recognizable language, customs, and rituals. Many of the key features of the program are so familiar and common in U.S. culture that they have achieved the level of cliché as evidenced by

Rising from the Dead
© 2007 by The Haworth Press, Inc. All rights reserved.
doi:10.1300/5800_02

bumper stickers reading "Easy Does It" and "Honk if you are a friend of Bill W." AA meetings often begin with a story, that is, a speaker tells her story and subsequent discussion focuses on ideas that the story contained. AA stories are told in a formulaic way and it is common to hear members assert that God speaks through the storyteller, thus the storyteller is of no consequence. Story is seen as a vehicle—what holds the transcendent meaning. Transcendent meanings are embedded in the individual story.[2]

This tradition is reaffirmed at individual AA meetings through spoken reading of the text that illustrates the formula. In the introductory remarks in Chapter 5 of the Big Book of Alcoholics Anonymous, members are advised to tell how it was, what happened, and how it is now. It is very common for this excerpt to be read at the beginning of AA meetings and this is one way that new members are instructed about the construction and transmission of story. Chapter 5 states, in part

> . . . *Our stories disclose in a general way what we used to be like, what happened, and what we are like now* [Italics added]. If you have decided you want what we have and are willing to go to any length to get it—then you are ready to take certain steps. At some of these we balked. We thought we could find an easier, softer way. But we could not. With all the earnestness at our command, we beg of you to be fearless and thorough from the very start. Some of us have tried to hold on to our old ideas and the result was nil until we let go absolutely.
>
> Remember that we deal with alcohol—cunning, baffling, powerful! Without help it is too much for us. But there is One who has all power—that One is God. May you find Him now! Half measures availed us nothing. We asked His protection and care with complete abandon.[3]

Within this process members tell and retell their stories, and within this structure a new sense of self is crafted.

One might pose the question of relevance here. What is the point of telling the story over and over again? Couldn't this even be counterproductive, even toxic to the storyteller? The answer to this question can be found in the stories themselves. Recovering women learn to speak to one another through the subtext of story.[4] In this way story becomes a kind of language of the heart in which personal story carries more abstract ideas such as the possibility of recovery, the reality of God's love, and the sacred significance of the individual in the eyes of God. Sociologist Ronald Takaki writes powerfully about the meaning of story for the teller and for the listener: "The telling of stories liberates. . . . After she escaped from slavery, Harriet Jacobs wrote in her autobiography, "[My purpose] is not to tell you what I have heard but what I have seen—and what I have suffered."[5] *AA women tell their stories so that others will be able to speak, so that other women will be able to tell what they have suffered.*

This is a critical element for helping professionals to grasp. Individual stories are shared so that the other can be heard. This is a dynamic embodiment of what theologian and educator Nelle Morton was describing when she wrote, "We began hearing one another to speech. We experienced God, as Spirit, hearing human beings to speech—to new creation. . . . We live out of our images; not out of our concepts or ideas."[6]

This process of story as concrete container of God's grace is evident in the excerpted transcripts that follow. We will consider three illustrations of recovery stories utilizing the formula as prescribed in AA—tell how it was, what happened, and how it is now.

HOW IT WAS

Alcoholic women are introduced to the unique brand of spirituality found in twelve-step programs immediately upon entering sobriety. Newcomers are taught to begin reconstructing their image of self through the creation of a life narrative that is inclusive of how far they fell and how much they want to return from beyond the pale. Indeed, the entirety of twelve-step spirituality is encoded in story construction. First, the newcomer tells others how it was.

I met MB in the first months of my research. She had achieved forty-three years of sobriety the summer we first spoke. We met in the same church basement where AA meetings are held and she recited her recovery story as she had done innumerable times before. This is her account of life during the development of her alcoholism.

> I had a mother who was an alcoholic and a father who was an alcoholic. And my mother was a very visible drunk. My father was less visible but his behavior was far more damaging to me. Let me mention my

mother first. My mother, who I say was a falling-down drunk, was actually a wonderful woman. She didn't drink, smoke, and yet later, after she was married to my father, he ran with a very heavy-drinking crowd and I guess after listening to the jokes, and all the dirty jokes, and all of that, I understand that finally she did pick up a drink. I think her father had been an alcoholic, by the way. And she picked up a drink and almost immediately triggered the alcoholism. She had a drastic reaction to it at first and her drinking was not pretty. That's the way that went. But I often think when I think of women that here was a wonderful person who was actually the scapegoat here. This was back in the days when being a drunk was considered being unladylike and so we all looked down on her. This was before I ever picked up a drink and had any understanding of the disease. I thought she could stop if she wanted, and things like that.

As I said, my father's alcoholism was very damaging to me. There was abuse, sexual abuse, but it got so bad that I was just absolutely terrified and just finally came to the point that I was afraid to come into the house, come home from school, all that kind of nightmare existence that women have that no one really understands. Certainly in that time no one would have believed a young girl had she come forward. You just stuffed it as well as you could. I finally just came to the point that I tried to commit suicide a number of times. My bedroom was on the third floor and I can remember sitting on the windowsill with one leg outside and thinking if I could get one leg outside the window, and I would look down on the retaining wall below and I just couldn't get the courage to let myself go and fall down. I just couldn't find the courage and of course that fed the shame. I was just so ashamed that I didn't think it was worth living. I tried it on one or more occasions and finally gave up and did what gals do and built a shell around myself. An iron shell. I used to call it a cocoon but it certainly wasn't any warm fuzzy cocoon. It was like an iron shell of closing out the world and closing off the feelings. And I couldn't feel bad things and of course couldn't feel good things either. I was a zombie long before I took my first drink.

Readers may find this to be a dramatic account, yet it became clear during the telling that MB did not find it to be so. Her story was delivered in a matter-of-fact way that belied the horror of her childhood situation. Her dispassionate delivery did not detract from the drama of her life story. This is a terrible story, yet she told it so that women who still suffer might know that there is a way out for them. She told her story to me so that other women would know that no matter what has happened to them, they could find solace in the company of women who can receive and cope with their stories. MB's story is an excellent example of storytelling as search and rescue. She offers this story when she speaks in AA meetings so that newcomers will know that details such as these can be remembered, recounted, and reconciled.

WHAT HAPPENED

Women who are new to recovery soon learn that the second part of story construction is to tell others about the events that precipitated their move into recovery—what happened. This element of story construction is perhaps the most familiar to pastoral counselors, because it includes an intuition of Divine intervention and grace more explicitly than accounts of how it was. The account of what happened is perhaps easier for newly recovering women to tell because it is actually where their felt-story begins. It is a truism that we consider our life stories from the center out—from the vantage of a "what happened" experience. Psychologists and theologians refer to these experiences as limit experiences because they introduce a sense of randomness and fragility to a life lived in ordinary time.[7] For the alcoholic woman, this is the first moment of her journey out of fractured, hellish time to sacred time.

NH gave the following account of her move from hell to reconciliation. Although she had thirty-two years of sobriety at the time that she related this story, the account was still fresh enough to prompt tears. This is her account of what happened.

This sober woman came from New York City. Her parents were celebrating their fiftieth anniversary so she came out. It was my husband's cousin and so he warned me. We had all done up nice to go to church and my children and everybody was bright and clean. I had my Dexedrine so I was very outgoing! And so he said, "Well, you're not going to like my cousin." And I said, "Why not?" And he says, "Well, she's a member of AA. She doesn't drink." And I said, "Well, that doesn't bother me. What do I care?" He said, "I just have a feeling that it's not going to go well for you." I said, "Well, I'll avoid her then!" I remember that we started drinking and partying in celebration of this couple's fiftieth. This woman just kept watching me and I thought that he was right, I don't think I like her; she is staring at me all the time. And somewhere along in that early hour or so of that gathering I must have just kind of given up. [She laughs.] I had no ... well I have no will when I am drinking except one that's not good! So I remember she came up to me and sat down on a stool. I remember she was sitting lower than me and she

> asked if she could talk to me for a few minutes. And I said "Sure." She
> said, "Why do you drink?" Well, it was the first time, I think, that anyone
> had ever asked me that. I can't remember that. I remember yelling but
> she was not that way. She was gentle and she said, "Why do you
> drink?" And something kind of broke inside me, you know, and I said,
> "Because I can't stop" [Her eyes tear up and the tears slide down her
> cheeks]. I get real emotional even now.

The beauty in this account is that the anonymous woman who spoke to NH took care to approach her in such a way that her defenses were not engaged. The woman is anonymous, yet clearly a person with a towering presence, thus giving a luminous quality to this story. In her engagement with NH she shifted the focus from the terror of alcoholism to the promise and possibility of redemption. For alcoholic women this is the critical difference—personal story is shaped, crafted, made as a kind of sacred container for the story of the other. The central truth to storycrafting in twelve-step recovery is that stories are containers. They call forth and hold the pain and suffering contained in the life of the other.

HOW IT IS NOW

The third element of story creation for alcoholic women is identification of how life now differs from life then. How is life in sacred space different from life in hell? Recovering women tell this part of their stories as a way to live into the reality of God's grace in their lives. This feature of the life narrative contains hope—the hope that a different life, a different self can emerge. One important feature of this part of alcoholic women's stories is that they include accounts of pain and suffering equally as painful as those found in accounts of how it was. The "how it is now" stories hold a different reality and thus a different interpretation of painful life events.

MH had twenty-five years of sobriety when she told me her story. Her life narrative includes accounts of child abuse and abandonment severe enough to shatter and cripple. In this excerpt the theme of abuse reappears as she tells about her experiences in recovery, and her account of her life now.

> And everything changed from there. It was never easy. I literally walked
> away from my family. I had $500 to my name, and an old station wagon

that was rusted out, and I went on the adventure of my life, knowing and trusting that it would be okay, because I am doing the right thing, and if I listen. These were very good things, and I've been blessed all along. I have had so many people in my life who have taken care of me when I was incapable of taking care of myself, that have loved me and breathed life in my soul. I have had so many magic miracles. To deal with my grief issues and get those behind me.

   . . . So I was doing the AA thing and working in the field and developing a support system but I knew that I had stuff going on inside of me. So I thought it might be a good idea if I started seeing a therapist. I was sober probably about two years and I chose to do that because I knew I needed help. And that's the first time—other than going into AA—I knew that I needed help with the conflict and the pain and everything inside. And I went to a therapist for the first time. I was sexually violated by the therapist. I was so green; I was so vulnerable; I was so little. I felt little. I just kind of cracked open my life. This whole, of course, intimacy happened. [She sighs. There is a silence.] The only reason I'm really talking about that is the violation of trust. I was so ready to deal with stuff and be open and whatever and that was violated. So I go back in and I deal with the shell and I hide and feel shame and keep it secret. I keep it inside myself and spin it all around really truly not realizing that it was sexual violation. All the time I'm thinking I'm responsible. . . . And I don't want to discount the sexual violation but the real violation was the professional relationship and the trust. Trust was never a big thing for me—I mean it's a very big thing but it's never been an easy thing because of what I have said. I take my time and I have learned now through sobriety and recovery who to trust and who not to trust. I trust my instincts and I have learned to do that. I have learned to take my time and respect that place inside me because it has never steered me wrong. That's again, part of the story. There's no bad news; it's all part of the story and it got me to who and where I am now. . . . It is a spiritual journey and it has been a spiritual journey and that's what it has all been for me. Just keep going to the light, and if I don't see the light pretend that it's there or hope that it's there because it's going to be there, because it's always taken care of you.

The amazing thing about MH's story is her willingness to live into a future of hope and trust in the face of the devastating effects of therapist sexual abuse. This account of survival is a result of Divine grace. No human power holds the capacity to heal wounds this deep.

WEAVING A SACRED CONTAINER

   Each week alcoholic women gather to tell their stories, to listen for the whisper of the Spirit in the voices of their sisters in recovery.

Newly sober women learn to craft their stories by attending to the silences of their sisters who are further along the path. As they grow in sobriety their accounts of "how it was" become shorter and a new awareness of the reconciling spirit of God is evidenced in stories of "what happened." As they journey toward long-term sobriety, accounts of "how it is now" offer solace and hope to those who are new to the path. This is the way of sobriety in AA.

What I find striking about the stories of all of the recovering women I have met is that their understandings of person, of suffering, and of God are spare, lean, and without frills. They often come to a conversation about spirituality having thrown off ties with traditional religion. In this way, their practiced spirituality could be said to be trans-religious. It is forged from a set of life experiences so shattering and dislocating that they drop the woman to a level deeper than everyday "ordinary time" spirituality. Theirs is more like triage spirituality, invoked during the equivalent of a battle or war; we might call this a soul war. As women grow in sobriety and grow out of their broken lives, a tension is created between the old self and the new self. Long-sober women know that to forget is to tear off a part of the self and send it away. They live within this tension and in sobriety hold together their lives before, during, and after drinking. This kind of remembering is made possible by the sacred web of sobriety.

In one sense the preceding stories illustrate that but one overarching theme is found in recovery narratives, a grace in relationships and in community that sustains the individual in times and troubles that seem insurmountable. When examined closely several related themes seem to emerge, so closely interwoven as to appear inseparable: imagining a new life, imagining a new community, imagining a new vision of God. The experience of redemptive community rests on a necessary shift out of ordinary life to life within the framework of sacred time, where the light of Divine love sustains and pervades all relationships. In this context, the simple reaching out from one woman to another echoes that preeminent reaching out that Christians know as the life, death, and resurrection of Jesus. Although few of the women interviewed would have offered this interpretation, and few women in recovery would characterize their actions in this way, the similarity is so striking it is breathtaking. In a Christian context, the transformed life becomes a Christ light for the one who still suffers and the community serves as a reconciling force, enveloping and healing through sacramental care and affection.

I close this chapter with a story that AM told me about her travels after her entry into sobriety. AM celebrated thirty years of sobriety the summer we met. This story was offered after the formal interview had concluded; we were just chatting and I hadn't turned off the audio recorder. This is her account of an experience with AA members in Columbia:

> When I was newly sober and living in Florida—maybe about seven months—three men showed up at our meeting from Columbia. One of them spoke some English and the others spoke only a little, and at that time they didn't have Spanish-speaking AA meetings like they do now. So I made it a point to go up to them after the meeting to tell them we were glad that they were there and all that. And one of then wanted to know if we had a detox or anything like that. We did have one but it was run by the Salvation Army and you didn't get in there unless they scooped you off a sidewalk someplace. So I took this guy down and showed him the detox facility. Well, he went back to Columbia and they patterned it after this one that they saw in Florida. About three years later I had the opportunity to go to there and I went to the meeting—I called these guys and they wanted me to see the detox unit. It wasn't just detox; they had a regular treatment program too. They had taken my picture. They had my picture there in this detox unit. And they would take my picture and show it to the women and say, "This is the picture of an alcoholic woman in the United States." So at this point they had eleven sober women in Colombia and they had about four meetings. That was in 1973 or so.
>
> Q: Have you thought about the power of that event?
> A: [She laughs.] They said, "This is an alcoholic woman!" The guy traveling with me laughed; he thought it was the funniest thing!
> Q: Do you tell this story often?
> A: No! I haven't even thought of it. You know you go around to these different places . . . that's what I mean about it's nice to be anonymous. You have no idea whose life you are going to affect. And you don't need to know. You could make it an ego trip, but you don't need to know how you have made a difference. But that is what I mean about making an effort to show up at the meetings.

As I have kept company with the women elders of Alcoholics Anonymous, it has become clear to me that the recovery experience—broken woman being mended—is recreated nearly every day in AA groups and in informal conversations between new members and their more experienced sisters. They are like shadows in our communities—they give and heal and make the presence of God manifest without ever really calling attention to themselves. As AM said to me, it is more important to be present to someone's suffering than it is to call attention to how you have performed this act. Yet their healing presence is felt in our community—expressing love and support and God's healing grace through their fidelity to those who still suffer.

PART II:
WE COME TO BREAK THE BREAD

Chapter 3

From Story to Theory

My first "real life" experience of the theoretical underpinnings of recovery began in 1974. I was enrolled in a community college seeking a certificate in chemical dependency counseling, the terminal degree available in Minnesota at that time. My class was noteworthy because we were the last group to be admitted without requiring a year of sobriety. Many of my classmates were addicts with six to eight weeks of sobriety. A classmate jokingly referred to this experience as the instructional equivalent of being raised by wolves! We had entered the field of addiction counseling at a time of great innovation and change. Public drunkenness had been decriminalized and federal money had been appropriated for prevention and treatment programming.[1] As chemical dependency programs and services proliferated, concerns about the preparation and training of counselors began to surface. The traditional view that alcoholics are best counseled by recovering alcoholics was being replaced by a belief that recovery in itself is not adequate training. Counseling programs might continue to be based on the twelve steps of Alcoholics Anonymous, but counselors must have more than a "good AA program" as therapeutic training. Alcoholism treatment was becoming mainstream, and as treatment became more acceptable, treatment programs became more sophisticated.

This complex set of circumstances led to questions about the credibility and efficacy of traditional forms of treatment and introduced one of the key issues in alcoholism treatment both then and now, that is, how do we integrate and apply twelve-step principles within broader therapeutic models? Is it possible to integrate twelve-step principles and twelve-step spirituality into therapeutic modalities without compromising therapeutic standards? These questions led to the perception by some that addiction counseling is no more than reli-

Rising from the Dead
© 2007 by The Haworth Press, Inc. All rights reserved.
doi:10.1300/5800_03

gion dressed in therapeutic clothing. These questions are troubling because a dearth of confidence already exists between pastors and therapists; at best religion and psychology have struck an uneasy truce. This lack of trust can lead to complex questions for professionals practicing in the field of addiction, questions about the nature and meaning of suffering and the relevance of the counselor's story.

In this chapter we break open this multiplicity of relationships while attempting to retain a view of the whole. What is the relationship between my own story and the story of my client? How is my own sense of spirituality related to that of my client and how do these life meanings form the energy and experience Christians refer to as the "bread of life"? In Christian communities the experiential territories of life, death, and resurrection are traversed each year during the Lenten season. If we are to stay true to our plan to walk the path from Ash Wednesday to Pentecost, this next stage of the journey will take us into the wilderness. Desert metaphors are especially suitable here because the descent into active alcoholism and accompanying disintegration of normal life has much in common with the experience of being lost in a wasteland. Not a day hike, this is a wilderness experience where safe haven seems impossibly far.

THE MINNESOTA MODEL OF TREATMENT

The Minnesota model for addiction treatment came to prominence during the late twentieth century and it remains the dominant model for addiction treatment both in the United States and worldwide. It begins with an understanding of addiction as a primary, progressive, chronic, and fatal disease and its treatment strategies are an amalgamation of twelve-step spirituality and therapeutic principles. Rehabilitation programs that utilize the Minnesota model focus on healing the whole person through a course of treatment that includes total abstinence, education, and group support. Patients are required to come to terms with negative (drinking) behavior and its consequences for themselves and for those they love, stressing personal responsibility through a methodical personal assessment. The change process is reinforced by instruction about the disease, group counseling, journaling, meditational reading, and family meetings. Therapeutic insights are supported by attendance at twelve-step meetings and patients commonly work steps one through five of the twelve steps of Alcoholics Anonymous before being discharged. Upon completing treatment, patients participate in aftercare groups, in which new insights and behaviors are supported and encouraged by people sharing the same experience.

The Minnesota model utilizes the twelve steps, but it is not considered "spiritual" per se, and efforts are made to separate therapy, such as group or individual counseling sessions, from the practice of spirituality. Group therapy focuses on healing intrapersonal and interpersonal relationships. The fifth step, the process in which the alcoholic shares the fullness of her drinking history, is done with chaplains or AA sponsors, not with therapists. A fair amount of debate about the role of spirituality and twelve-step language is found in such programs. Treatment centers advertising themselves as alternatives to twelve-step treatment have proliferated and numerous Web sites are devoted to debunking the "cult" of twelve-step spirituality. These are the bald facts.

Lurking below the surface of this model is an experience far more mystical than is apparent on the surface. Chemical dependency counselors facilitate a process of recovery that is, for all intents and purposes, impossible. The ravages of alcoholism are well documented and recovery rates do not inspire confidence, yet counselors practicing the Minnesota model operate within a sphere of "hope for," that is, hope for the possibility of change where no change has seemed possible. Professor Brom Johnson, a pioneer in the development of counselor training programs describes the Minnesota model in this way:

> Patients engage in treatment activities with the goal being that they begin replacing a self-destructive lifestyle that was created by their addiction with a new self-affirming lifestyle called recovery. During their addiction patients acted in ways that caused them to deny, reject, and then finally abandon their true authentic selves. With that abandonment they also lost significant human relationships and their relationship with the Divine Mystery that sustains all. To help patients recover themselves, their relationships with meaningful others and their relationship with the Source of All, patients participate in an in-depth reflection of how their alcoholic behavior affected themselves and their loved ones. Although for most patients this is an extremely diffi-

cult and painful process, it is central to the goal of replacing self-deception with self-awareness.[2]

We can see in Johnson's description a relational approach to counseling that is infused with a sense of the numinous within the ordinary, an image of the counseling relationship that includes awareness of the God who calls us to community. Not a traditionally secular model of counseling, it is self-consciously spiritual. The tradition within this domain of counseling upholds that the therapist's story is fair game, a relevant piece of the equation, shared with the clients and often, with their families. It is a tool, a lens through which alternative modes of being and becoming are viewed. This relational awareness results in a kind of hybrid therapeutic mode or role somewhere between counselor and pastor. Addiction counselors who practice within the Minnesota model must be able to speak the language of mental health and the language of spirituality with equal facility. This mode of relating de-emphasizes the role of counselor as expert and emphasizes the role of counselor as sage or companion.

In this field I learned the deepest lessons about giving up the role as "expert." My best and most useful moments as an addictions counselor came when I was willing to relinquish being a counselor in order to become a companion or witness. I learned that there is little to say in the presence of that pain which comes from self-inflicted cataclysmic events. Some cruelty, some suffering, some missteps do seem to transcend the realm of mental health. As a new counselor I worked with a woman who was the picture of serenity and grace. Benign appearance notwithstanding, her most memorable line was, "In this business you have to have a sincere belief in the dead and the dying!" While working with her I met a man whose skin was the color of saffron or butter—no human being is meant to be that color. His liver and kidneys were failing but he had sought help too late. He died four days after I met him. My mentor and co-worker's ominous phrase expressed, I think, the reality of the life circumstances of the people with whom we were working. Her companion, a woman with an equally graceful demeanor, provided a counterpoint message. She was as certain of the possibilities of recovery as she was of death and taxes. Paraphrasing St. Teresa of Avila she told new therapists and interns and clients and anyone who would listen, "There is no defense against love!" I came to admire and cherish the spirituality of these women, and others with whom I worked. One of them frequently reminded me, "Every day my life reveals to me my closeness to or distance from God." She held her hands high, as if in prayer when she said this. It was her one-sentence philosophy of treatment.

Treatment centers that utilize this model of treatment inhabit a middle ground between the secular and religious world, no small feat because of an inherent difficulty in maintaining dual citizenship in worlds that are so different. Therapists working in alcoholism treatment must speak the bilingual language of therapy and spirituality with equal proficiency. In theological language we might say they balance precariously between the sacred and the profane.[3] This ability stands between worlds of experience and distinguishes this mode of counseling. How does this bilingual capacity assist in navigating the treacherous terrain of recovery? We begin in the Lenten wilderness.

ENTERING THE WASTELAND: REVISITING HOW IT WAS

Although it might seem that a description of the recovery process should begin with cessation of drinking, virtually all literature in the field of treatment and recovery begins with an account of myriad difficulties caused by alcoholic drinking patterns.[4] The onset of alcoholic drinking—not to be confused with nonalcoholic or "social" drinking—is virtually invisible. Those in the beginning stages of alcoholism appear to others to be in good health and essentially unchanged, yet the person has become changed in an essential and terrible way. A subtle shift has taken place whereby alcohol consumption becomes the focal point of the person's energies and attention. Family, friends, work, and other interests are neglected as the addict seeks solace in the fog of drinking. This causes a subtle shift in the person's cognitive processes. We can consider this shift as a move from ordinary time to extraordinary time because the normal counted days of everyday, ordinary small crises and resolutions are left behind. For the woman who has become a problem drinker, the ordinary is no longer available. In the language of the twelve steps, she has become powerless over alcohol and her life has become unmanageable (step one).

In an exceptional analysis of this complex process Stephanie Brown observes that when powerlessness and unmanageability reign, a kind of correspondence occurs between what the person believes and how she behaves. This congruence is the hallmark of alcoholic drinking and constitutes what Brown refers to as "the drinking stage." The woman drinker tells herself, "I am not an alcoholic. I can drink" and she does drink to excess.[5] Subtle and powerful defenses support this constellation of thinking and behavior, including denial, bargaining, minimizing, blaming, and rationalization.[6] This is an inherently "stable" situation because the woman's perceptions match her behaviors. This stability can appear to be paradoxical since alcoholism clearly leads to a destabilized life; however, the "felt experience" or internal experience of alcoholism is one of stable self-perception, and this is referred to as "sincere delusion."[7]

Of course it is well documented that those who must live with or deal with the drinking alcoholic have a radically different experience. AA literature describes the experience of the family in the following way: "The alcoholic is like a tornado roaring his way through the lives of others. Hearts are broken. Sweet relationships are dead. Affections have been uprooted. Selfish and inconsiderate habits have kept the home in turmoil."[8] Thus the family and friends of the alcoholic experience the tornadic effects of her developing alcoholic personality or persona, while she scrambles to preserve the public appearance and accompanying self-image of a controlled social drinker.

The problem of congruence takes center stage for the woman who is in the beginning stages of alcoholism. Congruence simply means that a relationship exists between what is happening internally versus what is happening externally.[9] Am I aware of how I am behaving? Do my internal beliefs match my external actions? C.S. Lewis has written poignantly about our very human need to maintain a good public image. He wrote, "We regret that we are the people we find ourselves to be" which means that we regret all of those ordinary dishonesties and image-maintenance activities that prevent our more craven selves from being seen.[10] Facing demons is part of the normal and necessary struggle to achieve self-actualization. Authentic selfhood is not attained without struggle and volumes have been written about the shadow self and the search for authenticity. Although issues of image maintenance and control are as much a function of ordinary life as the urge to seem humble, or good, or any other attribute that serves to preserve a good image, this is a pale version of the need to be in control experienced by the alcoholic.

It is impossible to overstate the terror of loss of control that is the consequence of alcoholism. Once this awareness has dawned, the alcoholic must immediately repress it and focus on the perceived defects of others. Our natural propensity for self-defense becomes distorted by this experience of powerlessness and the frantic urge to remain in control, and to seem to others to be in control, rises out of the terrible existential realization that control has been irrevocably lost. This terrifying insight must be avoided at all costs. When the alcoholic woman becomes "a tornado," her defenses are utilized to block and then alter her perception of this reality. This motive of sincere delusion causes a "sincere" belief that nothing is wrong.[11] With the onset of this behavior, the drinker often wonders secretly if she is going insane (step two).

At this stage the alcoholic has lost all control over negative behavior and she has a vested interest in denying the effects of this behavior on others. In this way alcoholic women can seem particularly obstinate, difficult, and profoundly unsympathetic, which leads to a dangerous matrix of estrangement and self-loathing. Alcoholics can be among the most problematical and the least sympathetic of clients. In blunt terms, women alcoholics, as with their male counterparts, behave badly and give the appearance of caring little about the consequences of their actions. Thus the alcoholic woman begins to inhabit a profoundly isolating and terrifying existential wilderness.

The following stories are distressing examples of the wilderness experience. NH told this story about her erratic and dangerous behavior during drinking binges.

> I caused a lot of trouble. I used to take my clothes off in public. I have no conscious memory of it at all but I know I did it because I had to face it the next morning. I would fight with the LAPD [Los Angeles Police Department]; literally fight. I had to go to jail on a DUI. And I do remember yelling at the attendant, "You can't put me in there! I'm a mother!" And she said, "Well, you're a DRUNK mother!" And she gave me a big push and in I went! And my husband came down several hours later, I'm sure he felt he would let me cool it. That didn't help our marriage either.

PK had this to say about her experience as a foster parent. In this excerpt the disconnection between her intentions and her actions are cast in stark relief.

During the first five years of our marriage we had a foster child who was placed with us because he was living in a household where his mother was mentally retarded and alcoholic. So he ended up in a family where people were very intelligent and alcoholic, so I don't know how much difference it made! We were still maintaining then at that time. My ex-husband was also diagnosed with manic-depression and the only reason that I bring that up is that it throws a lot of discord into the mix when he would medicate with alcohol. So my thing was to . . . [Her voice trails off]. I guess I drank to escape, for all the obvious reasons, and then I just drank because it felt good. It felt better than feeling the way that I felt.

Finally, MB recounted her experiences with her adopted daughter. She told this story in a calm and measured way in the hope that women who suffer from addiction would see that they are not alone, that others have traveled the wilderness territory of loss of control.

I would sit in church hung-over and reeking of alcohol and one day our pastor said that they were looking for homes for children from broken homes. These were children who had been taken away from their families, from their parents because their parents were alcoholic and unable to take care of them. It was like a flashbulb going off and I thought, "That's what I need. I need a child, then everything will be all right and the players will be in place." And so I talked my husband into taking one. She came to us when she was three years, three months. That was the real beginning of my elevator life. She came into my life at three months before Christmas. They told me not to buy any clothes because she would come with all her clothes and her toys and so forth. I remember I had to drink an extra amount that day to get ready for this extra responsibility. And she came to the door and all she had with her was just a brown grocery bag and after supper I can remember very vividly—and I really never want to forget it—standing at the dining room table looking for something to put her to bed in and I pulled things out of the bag one by one. I finally found this little jersey nightie, this little infant's nightie that just had been allowed to stretch with her body. It was all full of holes and gray. And I said, "Can you imagine putting a child in anything like this?" Yet the things that I was going to do to that little girl in the next few years were so much worse than putting her in an old nightie. Finally a couple of years later the symptoms got so bad—and I never used to talk about this at meetings, but I do now because I find that there are so many women who can relate to it—things got so bad that I began to want to strike out at people. I know today that what that was, was hating myself so much and if the mailman came to the door I might want to hit him. That was scary! It got to the point that if my little girl would come into the kitchen and I was peeling potatoes I would have to throw that knife on the counter because that was how afraid I was. That was when she was going to school and she had a long ponytail. I can remember sitting at the dining room table combing and brushing her hair and all of the sudden that compulsion would just come over me to strike out. I really didn't want to hurt her and so I would push her away and throw the brush down and walk around for a while until it passed.

The sadness in these accounts is terrible in its inevitability, highlighting the deep despair that alcoholic women live with as their drinking progresses. The life of an alcoholic woman is truly nightmarish and members of AA habitually tell newcomers that the drinking alcoholic has but three options: quit, die, or go insane.

These stories are illustrative of a web of action/reaction that traps the alcoholic into an unavoidable set of consequences, all of them disastrous. The circumstances detailed here lead inevitably to questions about the ultimate worthwhileness of life. Alcoholic women are driven, through their actions when drinking, toward a collision with the most elemental questions posed by life. This image of being driven to a collision with the nature and meaning of life resonates for Christians with the Gospel of Mark, in which Jesus is sent into the desert by the Spirit and tested for forty days (Mark 1:12-13). Moreover, these questions document the inherent difference between ordinary time and extraordinary time. The alcoholic woman asks herself such elemental questions as, "What is truth? What is authority? To whom do I listen?"[12]

AN UNLIKELY OASIS:
REVISITING WHAT HAPPENED

Just how deep can the pain go before it becomes terminal? Researchers who study addiction note that it is unclear what exactly happens to cause a change in the behavior and thinking of the drinking alcoholic. Stephanie Brown refers to this shift in perception as the "transition stage," and AA refers to it as "hitting bottom," that is, the person moves from drinking to not drinking.[13] This shift in behavior can be triggered by a random event, such as a comment that finally hits home or a situation that strikes the drinker in a new and disturbing way. This interruption is so difficult to categorize, control, or fabricate because the event that destabilizes the alcoholic's pattern of thoughts/behaviors is likely to be one so similar to others as to be in-

distinguishable from "life as usual." Those who love the alcoholic are
left wondering why *this* event or comment at *this* time causes a fundamental shift in her perception of herself and of the world, when the
same type of event or comment at another time had no discernable effect at all. Hitting bottom means an essential re-ordering of the sense
of self-in-the-world, at its essence a conversion experience.[14]

AA literature notes that surrender, or "hitting bottom" is the central
feature of this shift in behavior.[15] Vernon Johnson, a pioneer in the
development of the Minnesota model, taught that families and friends
of the addict can assist with this process through direct intervention—a process of loving confrontation designed to present the addict with a clear picture of her drinking, thus shattering her denial
long enough for her to see the need for treatment.[16] For the alcoholic,
hitting bottom is the profoundly dislocating experience of waking up
and realizing that the nightmare is real. Hitting bottom includes a
crippling awareness of the depth of the loss of control, a painful
awareness of the ways in which values and beliefs have been compro-
mised, and an experience of psychic and spiritual vertigo both breathtaking and potentially fatal. PK's story about her last drunk is a classic "what happened" story.

> We went out to a party and of course we started it the way we started
> all parties, we started drinking early. I sent the children—because we
> still had our foster child and my son was four years old at the time—I
> sent them over to my mother's house for an overnight because we
> were going to this big going-away party for a friend of ours who was
> moving. So we didn't have a car at the time because financially we
> were always in trouble. We started drinking, which was fine because
> we figured we wouldn't be driving drunk! [She laughs.] And we got on
> the bus and went over to Minneapolis, drunk. I mean it was just horri-
> ble; it was inconceivable to me that I could physically drink that much. I
> went into a blackout for three hours and continued to drink. I had never
> had that happen to me before that I drank so much that I didn't sober
> up for two days. And I woke up that Sunday and I don't know why or
> how but it was a beautiful Sunday morning in September. We had a
> third floor apartment; there was sun everywhere. I was all alone and
> didn't know where my husband was and I just sat up and had the most
> incredible experience of fear in my life. It was physically chilling; it was
> as though I was sitting in a cold spot. And I sat there and sat there; I
> don't know how long I sat there but it was a long time. I was just unable
> to move. I can remember getting up and going into the kitchen and call-
> ing my mother. I had no . . . I knew my mom was in AA but I didn't know
> what it was or why it was. I thought it was just a kind of hokey group of

folks. And she went down to this place in downtown St. Paul to this place that was sort of dingy and ugly and all those people were gutter drunks and . . . why was my mother there? Hmmm? [She smiles.] So I called and I said, "You know, Mom, I think I have a problem. I think I need to go to a meeting."

When the alcoholic woman experiences hitting bottom, the congruence between her self-image and her behavior—a congruence that she had carefully guarded during the drinking stage—is thrown off balance.[17] Hitting bottom causes an unexpected possibility of safe harbor from the constant storm of self-loathing and self-recrimination. From a spiritual point of view we might say that a sudden inbreaking of grace and possibility accompanies this destabilization (step three). It is interesting to note that although this fracture in the denial system can be *described,* it cannot actually be *explained.* The noetic quality evident in these stories defies theoretical description.[18]

PJ offers the following account of change that illustrates the elusive and almost mystical quality of the experience of hitting bottom.

I called AA in a blackout. I barely remember two lovely ladies coming to see me. One of them even washed my hair and fixed me all up. I vaguely remember all this. And that night they came back and took me to a meeting. No. I drove myself to the meeting because I stopped by a bar and had a couple of drinks before I went to the meeting. That's the only way I got there. They tell me—there's not too many people around now that were at my first meeting but the ones that were tell me that they had to hold the table down because I shook so bad. But you know I don't remember hardly anything about that meeting except that feeling of that there was some hope there. And that if I came out and said I was an alcoholic I could be helped. And so I did. I came home and I had some beers left; I used to hide them in a suitcase in a garage. I had three beers left in the suitcase. Of course they were warm but I'm English so I'm used to warm beer. So I drank them, went to bed and never had another drink afterwards. The urge to drink was almost immediately lifted from me. I never had any religious education but I had to know that my Higher Power was working for me even when I couldn't work for myself. I mean, he was the one that dialed that phone for me and sent those two ladies to see me. And that's how I got into AA.

PK's and PJ's last drunk accounts are classic "hitting bottom" stories, that is, they are experiences that might not have resulted in the move to sobriety had they happened on another day or at a different time. Both women possessed denial systems that were solidly in place. What can we possibly make of this shift? The women who gave their stories for this book, without exception, identify God as the initiator of their change of heart: God has placed the helper in her path; God takes charge of the timing; God dials the telephone. One of the most interesting and compelling aspects of twelve-step recovery is the notion that God will do for the individuals what they cannot do for themselves.[19]

This shift of focus is particularly instructive for those in the helping professions because psychotherapeutic models tend to be intrinsically secular and thus consciously self-limiting. The limits of such theoretical models are especially evident when considering patients who hit bottom. Clinical models inform us of the "how" of transition but spirituality addresses the "why." As we have already seen, programs based on the Minnesota model utilize conceptual categories that allow them to navigate the space between therapeutic language and spiritual language. They are able to employ both sets of language and consequently have the capacity to accommodate questions of "how" and "why."

Their unique contribution to the helping professions is that they are at home with the language of recovery, a language that tolerates and even encourages the language of the Spirit. The strength of this language lies in encouragement of a sense of human relationships supported by Divine relationship, particularly poignant when seen in the efforts of families intervening with loved ones who suffer from alcoholism. When facilitated with care, intervention into the drinking behavior allows loved ones to interrupt the destructive pattern of drinking while maintaining sure footing in the belief that entry into recovery cannot be "controlled."

FINDING THE SURE PATH:
REVISITING HOW IT IS NOW

When women enter recovery they begin to reconsider their stories within the context of a program of spirituality. All of the actions in early sobriety are focused on discovering a new answer to the questions, "What is truth? What is authority? To whom do I listen?"[20] A new story is crafted as she discovers answers to these questions. Sobriety medallions, and other tangible signs of progress mark growth and progress.[21] Women who are new to sobriety begin to tell and retell their life stories, re-imagining their stories and the meaning behind them. At thirty days, sixty days, ninety days, six months, nine months, one year, two years, etc., her story is revisited, new awareness is integrated, and a kind of re-cognition (or recognition) takes place.[22] People secure these new awarenesses through use of sobriety tokens, which serve as concrete reminders of sobriety benchmarks.[23] The net result is that people begin to integrate the prior negative and tragic choices into new life narratives, which contain the seeds of hope.

What is the goal of this new life story? The stories I collected suggest that new narratives make new life-meanings, that is, new meaning related to the suffering caused and the suffering experienced. In this kind of storycrafting recovering people find a way to make the suffering mean more than a life wasted; one's life is put in service to something greater than the individual self. The new life story leads to a mandate to serve others. In fact, written on the wall of innumerable AA clubhouses and gathering places is the credo, "I am responsible. If anyone anywhere reaches out for help, I want the hand of AA to be there. And for that I am responsible." A new fabric of meaning is stitched—one day, one hour at a time. This new life story with its inherent spiritual base forms the gestalt of a new personality, a truly new life.

The stories I received are full of examples in which service to others becomes a necessary element of a new life in recovery. Two illustrations may be helpful. NH told this story:

> I started going to all these meetings and I didn't have to drink again for fifty-seven days. And that's pretty amazing to a daily drinker. I liked the people as well as I liked people at all. I made myself be out of myself. They still washed cups in those days [before coffee was offered in Styrofoam cups]. So my friend and I would go—again, like I told you, my nature—if I think that it is benefiting me I can make myself do things—so I would make myself go in the kitchen. So this one lady who became my sponsor, she passed by me one day in the window—there was one of those service windows in the kitchen—and she looks in and says, "It beats talking to people, doesn't it!" And it is so true! I didn't want people to get close to me; I didn't want them to know me. I didn't really feel like I wasn't worthy or anything like that. I just didn't like that kind of thing. And I'm still a little bit like that. But because I had that will to do what I felt and wanted to be a part of it all I just would push myself out into AA and took on service jobs and began to make my life that way.

MB offered this account of her early sobriety:

> One of the things my sponsor said to me when I first came in, during the first couple of weeks was for me to get up in the morning and to say, "Thank God for the gift of life today and help me not to take a drink today." My bedroom was by a window and I would stand there and say in really angry tones, "THANK YOU, GOD, FOR. . . ." [She laughs] But I said it. And I can remember a few weeks later—and I had been physically sober, remember, for a few weeks—I felt a little tickle that starts up my spine and I realized that I was GLAD to be sober today. I wasn't in the bathroom throwing up. I was sober and it felt good. So I continue forty-three years later. I sit up and say, "Thank you, God, for the gift of life today." And I say it now with a different tone. And of course for me today the most important thing is the relationship with a Higher Power. He has just done so much for me. You have to get out of the director's seat. And it doesn't happen all at once, but it is a very gradual process. I remember I say most mornings, "Please take the big 'I' out of me."

Treatment centers based on the Minnesota model provide counseling and education that assists newly sober alcoholics in navigating these changes. As we have seen, once the newly sober alcoholic comes to terms with the idea that she is powerless over alcohol and her life is unmanageable (step one), she will realize that only a power greater than herself can restore her to sanity (step two). This leads to an action step. She must make a decision to turn her will and her life over to a Power greater than herself; in turning it over she recovers control (step three). What kind of control is restored, if previous attempts at control had such disastrous effects? Marvin Shaw describes this new mode in *The Paradox of Intention*. He writes that the restored sense of control is a function of existence rather than action, a "gift" rather than a destination or prize.[24] *In this view, control is restored through the process of telling a new life story.* Control is seen as a by-product of letting go. It emerges out of a willingness to be completely honest (steps four and five) and it restores the shattered soul by reorienting the self-in-the-world. The woman alcoholic begins the process of sobriety by asking, "What is truth? What is authority? To whom do I listen?" and in telling a new life story she comes to believe that a Power greater than herself has restored her to sanity and to a sacred path, a path out of the wilderness.[25]

Chapter 4

Descending into Hell: Shame and Guilt

A POVERTY OF SOUL

Not long ago I heard a homily based on a passage from the Gospel of Mark about Jesus and the rich young man (Mark 10:17-30). This scriptural passage tells the story of a prosperous young man who kneels before Jesus and asks how he might achieve eternal life. When Jesus enumerates the commandments the young man replies that he has kept them all. Jesus tells him that he lacks one thing—he must sell all that he owns and give it to the poor—and then he can follow Jesus. The rich young man goes away grieving. The homilist, a recovering woman with twenty-seven years of sobriety, noted the similarity between the wealthy young man and herself, a similarity of *internal reality* that overcame the apparent dissimilarity of prosperity and means. This is an excerpt from her sermon:

> As the child of two alcoholic parents and as a recovering alcoholic and drug addict I have had a firsthand experience with a certain kind of poverty. My parents' drinking ensured that there would not be enough. Not enough food, not enough clothes, not enough heat in the winter. We lived in a nice neighborhood, full of nice, middle-class people. Ours was the house that everyone commented on because it wasn't painted, wasn't kept up, wasn't maintained. My dad had a collection of broken cars that he kept in the driveway and in the backyard. Every so often the neighbors would call the city and he would get a citation. We were a family that was unraveling. I remember the year that the Salvation Army delivered food. They came in a marked van so there was no doubt as to who they were. And they carried boxes in—not out. So there was no doubt about who was on the receiving end of this donation. If they hadn't come, we would not have had a Christmas dinner. We were very grateful. And very ashamed. The box of food included almond bark. I haven't eaten it since. My own drug and alcohol addiction ensured that I would have an even more "up close and personal" expe-

Rising from the Dead
© 2007 by The Haworth Press, Inc. All rights reserved.
doi:10.1300/5800_04

rience with poverty. I lived a life of desperation—I was what is referred to as a "low bottom" addict. Now, here is what I know about poverty. It didn't make me feel noble. It didn't make me feel blessed. It just made me feel scared. And it made me feel hunted—like someone was chasing me. And, of course, it made me feel ashamed—deeply ashamed. I have spent the better part of my twenty-seven years of sobriety attempting to erase all signs, all indicators that I ever lived a life like that. When hints of my past peek out it is almost as if my emotional petticoat is showing. I have worked long and hard to smooth out all of my rough edges, to fit back into middle-class society. I live in a safe neighborhood and am married to a gentle soul who is profoundly and fundamentally nonviolent. I am off the streets.[1]

This excerpt provides a rich example of the complexity of the emotion of shame, especially when it occurs within the context of family alcoholism. It is impossible to consider the dynamics of addiction and recovery without mention of shame and guilt.[2] There are actually two levels of shame—ordinary shame and extraordinary/catastrophic shame. Even ordinary shame has awesome and terrible characteristics. Shame stops time. What other emotion can make such a claim? Love and hate can make time seem either exquisitely short or agonizingly long. Only shame stops time completely. A temptation arises to treat shame at a distance is perhaps because writing about it in the particular—my shame, your shame—is so painful that to do so seems foolhardy. Consider one shameful moment from your own life. How willing are you to share it? What has to happen internally before you can bring yourself to disclose it?

This feature of the dynamics of shame makes the stories of recovering alcoholic women so compelling. Their shame is so healed, so reconciled, so redeemed that they share it willingly in order to reach out to others who suffer. Sobriety narratives are healed narratives. The sober alcoholic woman possesses a story that has been transformed through the grace of God's healing love (steps four and five). This healed story then provides the means through which others find the courage to tell and then claim their own stories. If the newly sober alcoholic wants to tell a new life story, then shame and guilt must be healed or the story will retain the power to destroy the teller. For long-sober alcoholic women, shameful stories have become transformed into vehicles for change—the shameful event has lost its power to injure. A new story is told, one in which the pain and injury of alcoholic drinking now represents the raw material for a transformed life. This is the power of shame within the context of recovery stories.[3]

Shame Defined

What is shame? Shame is the emotion that is experienced when a person feels herself to be flawed in some crucial way. Shame is most uncomfortable when it happens in public, when the perceived flaw is apparent to all who take the time to look. Shame is a natural emotion, and like other emotions such as anger and sadness, is neither good nor bad. Shame may be uncomfortable, but it is not harmful to the self unless it begins to take over ordinary life and ordinary time. Commonplace shame, like other feelings, has survival value. It aids our understanding of ourselves as finite, limited creatures. Applying theological categories we would say it reminds us that we have been created as imperfect beings who have the capacity to imagine perfection but who can never achieve it.[4]

We can think of shame and embarrassment as part of the same continuum, with extreme, debilitating, catastrophic shame on one end and mild embarrassment on the other. Embarrassment and shame are essentially the same emotion experienced in different degrees. A benign example of the experience of shame might be how we felt as children when the teacher asked us a question and we didn't know the answer. A second example might be when a teacher (whose bread and butter is her ability to think, speak, respond) suddenly mismanages a classroom situation. In both examples two things are happening simultaneously: the mistake has been noticed and the person feels caught and surprised by the situation; this is not a planned encounter. The natural consequence is to feel embarrassed or shameful because we feel as if all eyes are watching. Shame and shameful, embarrassing events happen, despite our best efforts to avoid them.

How can shame be considered benign, since feelings like the ones detailed previously can be so excruciatingly uncomfortable for children and adults alike? The truism already stated, that feelings are neither good nor bad, does seem to shed light on this apparent paradox. The feeling of shame, among other uncomfortable feelings, does give human beings something they need—a sense of limits. We know intuitively that it is not a compliment to say that a person is without shame. Such a state would make her dangerous to herself and others. To feel shame is to feel that the self is not without limits. A sense of shame in balance within the person is experienced as humility, that is, the person holds a realistic view of herself, including both assets and failings and all other elements that make a person human. In this way, then, shame need not be seen as dangerous or as an emotion to be avoided. While shame-as-humility is not always comfortable, it is definitely not dangerous. In fact, the elements of an ordinary shameful experience are almost identical to the elements of a very successful joke. Every joke has a story interrupted by a surprise. This is the experience of shame within the context of ordinary time.

CATASTROPHIC SHAME

Shame occuring over a long time or in repeated patterns becomes debilitating and dangerous to the person's identity.[5] Extreme debilitating shame is dangerous and toxic. It shackles individuals who experience it and they become unable to see the real world. Extreme shame can pose difficulties for the person in all relationships because it tends to be hidden. The hidden nature of shame can be seen in an illustration. During a weekend trip to the grocery store I witnessed the mother of a toddler react to the child's request to be held and comforted in this way: the mother recoiled from the child in contempt and snarled at her to "stop sniveling and walk like a big girl; big girls don't cry or hold hands." If this message is repeated, the girl will experience shame whenever she feels the need to be comforted. Those who love her may not be aware of this experience because it will be hidden from view. When they reach out to comfort her, a natural reaction, they will be rewarded with the defenses associated with shame. This process is often seen in alcoholic family systems and its effects can be catastrophic.

Catastrophic shame brings time to a standstill; when the person experiences catastrophic shame she is trapped in a crucible of self-loathing-made-public that is so agonizing it becomes life threatening. If we fail to appreciate this aspect of shame we fail to understand its relevance in recovery and healing. Virtually every woman who contributed to this book related an account of the devastating effects of catastrophic shame. FB told this story about her childhood, a powerful example of the power of childhood shame carried into adulthood.

> It seems that where I came from contributed a lot to where I got to and where I am today. It all does seem in a line of sorts. And I was thinking about, and thought that I should tell you that I was born into the four horsemen [of the apocalypse] or that's how I felt as a small child. I am

an adult child of alcoholics. I am an only child. My parents were divorced when I was three and my memories even to this day are not—and I have had much professional therapy and sobriety as well as step work in all the different twelve-step programs that we have—but my memories are just of terror, fear. Somebody mentioned that they bit their fingernails for a long time and I bit my fingernails until I was well past forty, and I think that says so much. I think it's interesting that my parents yelled at me about it but they never saw it as something that maybe needed looking into. So I think of myself as always on the outside looking in, which is why I really relate to AA because people there say that so often. My role in groups frequently was what I have come to know is the scapegoat role because I didn't know how to protect my boundaries or anything. I so wanted to be accepted but I would allow abuse. And I don't know now even looking back if I could have done different. I don't think so; if I could have I would have. I didn't know anything about life. I was too young to know that I should speak out, or whatnot.

DEFENDING AND DESPAIRING

The defenses associated with shame include rage, control, and perfectionism, and the reciprocal process of shame and defensiveness is well documented.[6] The crucial point for our discussion is the way that catastrophic shame successfully masks deep vulnerability, dread, and despair. Women who become alcoholic live out their lives within this constellation of emotions, yet the stories offered for this book are free of the defensiveness that so often accompanies the experience of shame. The recovering women elders I came to know were willing to step into the "spotlight" and tell their stories; they did not shrink from including details about the embarrassing and painful events from their drinking days.

MB, whose account of being sexually abused was told in Chapter 1, also described the process of shame linked to the abuse. She told this story about the effects of shame on her life as a young adult.

> I just put one foot in front of the other. I did go to school, I didn't make any friends, I didn't mix with the kids, I didn't have the dreams. I never dreamed about what I was going to do when I grew up or about getting married and having kids. That was not part of my life. I got through each day. That's all it was. I knew about that "twenty-four-hour" business before it saved my life in Alcoholics Anonymous. So I finally had an opportunity to leave that house—I wouldn't call it a home—to go to college and I can remember a brief moment of thinking things are go-

ing to be different—I am going to have a chance to live now. I remember feeling that momentary feeling of hope, and it was immediately extinguished by a drink of alcohol. I immediately came into contact with heavy drinking and I guess I would have to say that I immediately began drinking alcoholically. I never remember taking one drink and then not wanting more. I do believe that physical addiction to alcohol sometimes occurs much sooner than doctors might think and so I suppose it was with me. I hated alcohol. I hated what it had done to my mother. I hated what it had done to my life, and I knew what had done it. But once I began drinking—when we begin drinking we don't see what it does to us. At the very point where our drinking comes to the point where we need help we cease to see ourselves and that's the way it was for me. So right from the beginning I would have to say that I constantly ran from my drinking and the effects and consequences of my drinking. I remember burying all that stuff about my childhood and never talked to anyone about it.

We become most shameful when our most vulnerable thoughts and feelings are exposed publicly. One critical look can invite shame. It is in the eyes of those who witness our shame that our own weakness and failure are exposed to us. Human beings excel in the art of making others feel small and drinking alcoholics excel in the art of acting shamefully in public spaces. Since shame can fracture the woman's sense of self, recovery must include a healing of these fractures. We can see this kind of healing at work in the lives of the storytellers in this book. Paradoxically, healing takes place in much the same way that the initial shaming took place. Shame is healed through the act of "borrowing" the eyes of those who love you. Women new to sobriety practice seeing themselves through the loving eyes of women who have gone before them and it is within this process that they begin to see themselves more completely—not as flawed, but rather as naturally finite. Women new to recovery learn that to be limited is to be blessed.

MH offered an illustration of this process in this account of leaving home, describing the ways in which her uncle's love allowed her to see herself in a new way:

I had an uncle that was in the program and who I lived with after my mother died, for a year. A very beautiful man who was my mentor and I only lived with him one year. And when my mom would try to get sober she would leave us and go and stay with him. But then when she would come back to us, my father would pick her up and he would be drunk so then it would start all over again. So there were times when she would have four or six weeks of sobriety but she was never with us when that happened. After she died we lived there for a year. Incredible. I mean, it was like a mom-and-dad situation; it was safe, we ate, we had dinner, we had toilet paper. It was just unbelievable and you know, they became my mentors. The important thing is that I never wanted to disappoint them. And if I ever needed things, or really was going through anything I would talk to them. So when I had to make the decision about going to [another state] or not I made a special trip to go see them because I knew that whatever they would say would make sense. It would make sense and I was trying to make sense of insanity; I was walking a real thin line. So I met with them and I told them the scoop and he said to me, "You know, you deserve to be happy." And I looked at him and thought, "What in the hell are you talking about?" I mean, that didn't even penetrate. I mean I looked at him and I really couldn't get it—you deserve to be happy. Yeah, but my happiness is to make everybody else happy. But I knew that there was something that rang true and that I was twenty-one years old, I was an adult, and I had no idea how to take care of myself. I knew how to take care of everybody else. And I am responsible for my life and now the door opens. Are you going to go or are you not going to go? So I went. So being sober was one thing and making a decision to leave the insanity was another. To make a life of my own was the next decision. And those were the two major foundations I built my recovery and my sobriety on. Everything changed from there.

In contrast, MA muses on her continued feelings of isolation and shame, despite having achieved more than twenty-five years of sobriety.

With the people I work with now one of the first things I want them to figure out or know is that you can't do it alone, and you don't have to. Why would you!? But I don't remember anybody trying to tell me that. Maybe I wasn't ready to hear it. I also don't remember . . . and I am not saying my sponsors weren't good. I don't know that they were. They weren't good for me. That I know. I think I really wanted somebody to sponsor me who would say, "Now look, here is how we're going to do this." A woman who really sort of, not only sponsor me but mentor me. And I needed to know that that person would be there at two in the morning if I needed them and that I could call and not feel bad. And I never had that. It was like, "Yes I'll sponsor you but here are the times." Unfortunately, even today, if something is going on with me, it isn't going on between nine and five. In fact most likely doesn't. And so I am still sort of amazed that that whole thing worked for me and that I was still able to not use alcohol and to sort of get it.
. . . But I still would have to say I am struggling pretty hard. Sometimes I just can't work the steps—or maybe I'm not willing. I still suffer from a lot of guilt and shame and my guilt and shame is directly related

to how I am working the steps and directly related to my conscious contact, or lack thereof, I should say. So that when I get into a lot of guilt and shame then the spirituality part of my program sort of goes away and then something happens where I say, "Well, duh! I know what I am not doing." I still . . . yes, that's how it is. That's what I have to say. I'm done.

[The tape is turned off. MA says off-tape that perhaps she is not done and will return for a second conversation.]

I have been thinking about what I said the other day. I have been think-ing about the second step and being restored to sanity. And for me that was kind of neat because that must mean that at some point there was sanity in my life. I feel like—although I have moments where I don't now—but I have felt most of my life like I started broken, like that's ex-actly how I started. But as I thought about that it sounds somewhat pa-thetic to me. Maybe pathetic isn't the right word. I think that's pretty sad.

HEALING THE RIFT

Healing from shame is a deeply incarnational process in which re-lationships serve as a vehicle for change. As MA's story so poignantly reveals, when no loving support exists the person frozen in shame must expend untold energy to accomplish the healing process. It is not impossible to heal from shame using private spiritual exercises, but it is certainly more difficult. And this is where we can see a link between the secular process of treatment and the theological under-standing of God in the world, healing, reconciling, and reclaiming those that are lost and broken. How does this work? We can see the beginnings of this redemptive process when we consider how com-munal bonds heal both shame and guilt.

For alcoholic women, guilt becomes possible when shame has been healed. Sober alcoholics cannot really come to terms with per-sonal accountability until shame has been confronted and healing has begun. Out of the healed wounds of shame comes the ability to make amends for harms done to others and to oneself. Guilt emerges from a reexamined and reclaimed value system. Sober women learn to make peace with their past experiences by working the first five steps of Al-coholics Anonymous and they rebuild bridges to the ones they love by working steps six through nine.

Of critical importance to our discussion is the idea that healed shame actually leads to guilt; it leads to the ability to embrace the fullness of life in all of its moral complexity. Guilt heals shame by allowing us to make peace with reality. The stories of the elders whose stories grace these pages remind us that to disown our painful experiences is to depart from the possibility of connectedness; it is to remain in the wilderness of shame rather than risk connecting and being known. This link between secular models of healing and theological models is seen in the dynamic confrontation between Jesus and the rich man, and in the homilist's own dynamic confrontation with her flawed understandings of poverty and security.

Maya Angelou has written, "If you are made for the good, you do it without thinking."[7] Here is the key to the relational puzzle we are confronting. Drinking alcoholics build fortresses between themselves and those who love them. Without the healing reconciling encounters within the recovering community the danger exists that in sobriety they will erect a second fortress of false security. The stories we considered here illustrate the profound truth that making security into a kind of god leads to a potentially fatal poverty of the soul. Shame and guilt are not healed through the solitary endeavors of thinking or yearning and they are rarely healed through carefully cultivated security. Rather, they are healed through recognition of one's true essence or being, a recognition that cannot take place without the healing balm of community. The healing story, and the healed life this story represents, is resilient enough to accommodate all that the woman has been and hopes to be. This is the miracle of redeemed shame. It is the recognition of our true identities—we are made for the good. The woman who constructs such a story enters a new life made whole through the grace of the community. How this journey might be understood in more explicitly Christian language and symbols is the task for the remaining chapters.

PART III:
WE COME TO KNOW
OUR RISING FROM THE DEAD

Chapter 5

Standing Between Sin and Grace

FALLING IN LOVE

I began teaching theology in the summer of 1985. I had been work-ing as a therapist for nearly ten years and the majority of my clients were recovering women. My colleagues found my decision to study and then teach theology quite puzzling, in part because of their uneas-iness with religion and religiosity. I had initially shared their senti-ment because of the complex character of my childhood experiences. My parent's alcoholism had played out in a public way that included great commotion and embarrassment within our parish community. Some of my most painful childhood memories include drinking-re-lated catastrophes at church functions. It is a truism that anyone who works in the counseling field must first consider who she is trying to fix or save; in my years of working as a counselor I had decided that I would concentrate on "saving" myself and that continued interaction with the church of my childhood could not help with that healing. I had said good-bye to the church and thus was not at all enthusiastic about a theology course requirement.

I can remember, however, the exact moment that the subject grabbed hold of me. It was during my first semester as an adult non-traditional student. I had returned to college to finally finish my bach-elor's degree. I was sitting in a required theology class on Christian morality. It was the professor's intention to graph the account of the Fall of Adam and Eve as detailed in the book of Genesis. This was, he informed us, instructive about the human condition. The class was less than enthusiastic. I remember rolling my eyes and sighing deeply. I did not want to know what the Bible said about the human condition and I doubted that the professor's take on the human dilemma could match the light and fire of my own experience or that of my clients.

Rising from the Dead
© 2007 by The Haworth Press, Inc. All rights reserved.
doi:10.1300/5800_05

He forged ahead despite the less than enthusiastic reception from his students. Here is what he wrote on the chalkboard:

- We are creatures who know that we know. That is to say, we are self-aware.
- We can conceptualize both the idea of the infinite (this would be God) as well as the idea of the finite (this would be us).
- There is a problem for us here because although we can conceive of the infinite, we cannot really *be* it.
- Also, we can conceptualize a past when we were not, and a future when we will not be.
- This makes us *very* nervous—one might even say it makes us anxious.
- One response is to grab at everything and control it. This is called "sin."
- Another response is to let go. This is called "grace."

At that moment I fell in love. Here was a description of the experience of my clients—and of myself in some fundamental ways. In these sentences, and in the lecture that accompanied them, I recognized a tight articulation of the elementary principles invoked when counseling people who have been involved in the emotional equivalent of an apocalypse. My teacher was, of course, referring to some of the basic ideas in Reinhold Niebuhr's *The Nature and Destiny of Man.* I can remember checking the book out of the library and poring over the elegant prose. While the book proved too difficult for me to handle at that time, I had fallen in love with the beauty and logic of Niebuhr's ideas. I had enrolled as a social work major but I decided during my time in that class to leave the study of social work for study in theology. I was unwilling to let go of the order and beauty hinted at within the density of Niebuhr's thought.

During that Friday evening class I knew that I had seen, expressed in chalk dust, a piece of real truth. Here was the articulation of a set of ideas with which I had been wrestling in one form or another my whole life. I can see now, in retrospect, why I found these ideas so compelling. They capture the essence of suffering and redemption—and there is something almost mystical, I think, in using such spare language to describe such deep pain. I had left the church because I couldn't find a place there that felt safe, yet in the content of this class on theology I found a matrix of meaning that offered safe harbor. In retrospect, I have sometimes wondered if perhaps anyone who studies theology must also first consider who she is trying to save! I had finally found a theological "place" where I could enter a conversation with the God of my understanding and it has led me to a new understanding of God's saving, reconciling grace in the world. In this class I began the move from the secular work world to the work world of the Spirit. The language of theology provides a rich map for considering stories of falling and stories of grace such as those found in sobriety narratives.

As we have seen, recovery stories tend to inhabit the space between—between secular and religious, between heaven and hell, between lost and found. In this chapter we trace the path from secular story to sacred story. This is a departure from the traditional understanding of these stories, worth doing precisely because the symbols within the Christian tradition are so "sympathetic" to the process of narrative reconstruction described in preceding chapters. Prominent among the leaders in the development of the Minnesota model for treatment of alcoholism are ordained clergymembers such as Episcopal priest Vernon Johnson, founder of the Johnson Institute, and Lutheran pastor Phil Hanson, founder of Abbott Northwestern Chemical Dependency Treatment Unit. Their contributions to the field of addiction therapy most certainly contain elements from their own spiritual traditions. While the more secular models noted in Chapter 2 make no mention of sacrament and sacramental action, the elements of change they describe are rich with what Christians would recognize as theological and sacramental imagery.

Any discussion of Christian themes automatically raises questions about the nature of sin and its place in the experience of healing. Mention of the word "sin" makes the task more difficult. As we have already seen, religion and psychology have struck an uneasy peace and the introduction of the topic of sin does nothing to ease this problem. Why is this so? Perhaps because the catastrophic experiences in the sobriety stories we considered are full of situations that invite judgment. Alcoholics behave badly and society judges them for it. How can we navigate this difficulty? We can do it in part because of the nature of the stories we have been hearing; they are devoid of the defensiveness born of judgment. How do long-sober women understand the word "sin," how do they navigate within a traditionally male-dominated tradition, what is their image of God, and how do these various beliefs inform their life in community? In this and following chapters we examine the Christian language that seems most resonant with recovery experience.

LIFE AT THE THRESHOLD

Long-sober alcoholic women inhabit a space between the ordinary and the extraordinary. They somehow found solid footing in an experience that others might find daunting. Threshold metaphors are particularly suitable in discussions of the spirituality of sobriety because the movement from drinking to sobriety is so dislocating. Liminal experiences are essentially threshold experiences in which a breaking of the essential self results in a self made new. Systematic theologians such as David Tracy and Bernard Lonergan, and practical theologians such as Richard Rohr have considered the function of limit experiences within a life of faith. Descriptions of limit experiences are not the exclusive domain of theologians. Psychotherapists such as James L. Griffith, Melissa Elliott Griffith, and Robert Goodman have written about the radical depth of limit experiences and the spiritual relevance of limit experiences in psychotherapeutic relationships.[1] What do these writers have in common? They propose that "liminal space," the place where limits are experienced, is the necessary prerequisite to change; it is the fulcrum where God's grace breaks in and transforms.[2] Transformational situations such as the sobriety stories we heard are not ones that we would normally seek. This is part of what makes them so compelling. They are like a terrible walk in the wilderness where all familiar categories, all assumptions are brought into question. Here the gift of faith will be encountered—but at a tremendous price.

Threshold experiences share some characteristics with mystical experiences: they cannot be caused or controlled and they have a quality of ineffability.[3] And in order to endure such a place, an urgent need exists for the experience and guidance of those who visited it and survived. Like mystical experiences, threshold experiences have a kind of wrenching quality. Limit experiences are inherently struggle experiences.

How does this further our understanding of the nature of sin? Niebuhr's deft description of the experience of existential anxiety offers some assistance with this question. Sin can be understood as an attempt at control in the face of one's finitude. It is the created soul attempting to act as Creator. It is intense and cosmic pride. Recovering women inhabit a space in which their "sin" is confronted, in which where the concept of limit is introduced and then reinforced within the grace of a loving community. Long-sober women live a life of consistent assent to their own powerlessness.

This is one of the certain gifts offered by long-sober women who have crafted a new self in recovery. They entered liminal space and endured it. They came face to face with both sin and righteousness. And most important, they have lived *out of* this new knowledge of self for decades. This experience holds together the "ultimate paradox" of fundamental personality change. Rohr writes, "The truth is that I am radically different. The truth is that I am not different at all. And both of those are true at the same time."[4]

The critical difference between behavior changes made in ordinary time and behavior changes made in extraordinary time is in the outcome. Women who enter the threshold experience of hitting bottom emerge with their essential selves changed, a difference of *being*, rather than *doing*. Rohr cautions that being too good keeps the person from being made good.[5] In a repetition of the metaphor we considered earlier, Rohr writes "there might be nothing worse than being a nice little observant Catholic grain of wheat. It could keep you from becoming the bread of Christ."[6] This kind of radical change is evidenced by new descriptions of self. NH offered this account of the fruits of her sobriety.

> So it just began like that, just being gently led *here*, where we live. I believe that this *is* the spiritual universe. Now I know some people think it's where we're going, but because I've had consciousness change more than once, that's how I look at death, or ongoing life. It's like consciousness change. The world where we are is the spiritual universe. That's how I see it. So it's like the Scriptures, "The place whereon I stand is holy ground." I really believe that, because it has been witnessed to me so many times. We didn't have much money after all this story I told you—I needed to leave the bar business. So I went to work in the Alano club [AA club] where I had had that spiritual experience. And I managed that club for about eighteen months and I always just met the right people and was able to be of help, and see that I was of help. I'm a sober alcoholic and that's the best thing about me. It's what I have to offer.

Long-sober women exhibit familiarity with these threshold experiences; they speak about them with great peace and serenity. It can seem harsh to the casual observer, this experience of being driven from ordinary familiar spaces to the wilderness of brokenness and then remade and reshaped by the grace of God's love. Not for the faint of heart, yet a kind of calm emerges when one releases expectations that life will be agreeable, and if not agreeable, then not downright horrible. This is the abiding lesson learned in liminal space. KP tells about her life in later sobriety, which includes the death of her husband and her daughter's addiction to heroin:

> And when my husband died I had my two grandchildren living there because my oldest daughter was a drug addict. She would take anything that would make her feel good. That was it. And my youngest daughter moved to the West Coast and she got addicted to heroin and I was so afraid for her. I was so scared that she was going to die. And finally her boyfriend there called me and told me that she was so sick. One of my other AA friends had a husband who was an airline pilot and so she got to fly free. So she went out there and got my daughter. She had to stay there five days just to get her able to get on a plane. They got her home and brought her out in a wheelchair from the plane and I was afraid to hug her. She looked like somebody from Auschwitz. Her knees were huge and then she had these little bones sticking down, you know. It was terrible; it just broke my heart to see her. But she got okay and she went back to college. . . . So that was a happy ending. My oldest daughter was on the prescription drugs. She contracted cancer of the lung and she died four years ago. It will be four years on my AA birthday—four years on my sobriety anniversary! I thought, "Damn! You want to make sure I remembered when you died!" It was terrible and I wanted to die myself. I thought that when my first husband died that was the worst thing I had ever gone through. But when she died—and I knew she was going to die because they had no hope at all—I just wasn't ready for it. I thought I was ready but I wasn't. It took me a long time. And I didn't have to drink that time either.

KP can be peaceful in spite of the painful experiences in her lengthy sobriety. She saw this experience as a gift for women who are newer to sobriety—a message that difficulties and losses are not fatal. This might be the most amazing and beautiful aspect of the women who offered their stories for this narrative—that they continue to participate so completely in the process of being remade, reshaped in God's image.

One way to understand this process of letting go might be through the use of symbols and rituals that are fundamental to the practice of the Christian faith. When using this lens, AA might appear not as a fellowship, but as a sacred encounter that has the capacity to bring about elemental changes in the self, an entering of the Christ event to the extent that human beings can do so. Certainly it can be said that alcoholics spend the requisite days in hell.

Having encountered the internal change crafted within liminal space we are now ready to begin a discussion of how this experience informs our image of God and community, how feminist images of God expand our ability to navigate the experience of liminal space.

Chapter 6

Navigating Within Traditions

Recently a woman who is both colleague and friend asked me if it might hurt a woman's self-esteem to keep referring to herself as an alcoholic even though she had a bit of sobriety. The question was posed from out of nowhere– the kind of non sequitur that causes a conversation to tilt a bit. She went on to explain that this insistence on referring to sober alcoholics as "alcoholics" seemed like overkill, destined to ruin a woman's self-esteem and spirit. She knew that I had been interviewing sober alcoholic women and wanted my opinion on the subject. She raised an important point, one that has received a fair amount of attention by therapists, pastors, and pastoral counselors.

As I collected sobriety stories I was struck by the multitude of examples in which women had been shamed and mistreated by the men with whom they lived and worked and whom they loved and trusted. The examples were not restricted to the accounts of drinking behavior. Several women offered examples involving men in recovery who could not be counted on to act with their humanity solidly in place. In other cases, women in recovery who were engaged in service to the community experienced the vulnerability of public exposure. This is FB's account of a speaking engagement in which she participated after she had been sober a few years:

> After I had gotten sober I returned to that school where I had done the drinking. And it was alcohol awareness week at the school and they asked me to come and talk to the girls so I told my story. [She smiles.] And I am telling my story and this man comes up to me and he said, "After you told your story I knew who you were." And I asked him, "How do I know you?" because I didn't remember him. And he said, "I went out with you once." And I had to know the truth and I said, "Did we date very much? Did you ask me out again?" And he said, "No. You were an easy catch." [She looks away and sighs.]

Rising from the Dead
© 2007 by The Haworth Press, Inc. All rights reserved.
doi:10.1300/5800_06

Q: What did you think of his remark?
A: I didn't remember it. That was just unbelievable. It was a mean thing
   to say. . . .

The breezy cruelty of the man in question deserves no evaluation, however this account is illustrative of the kinds of responses women alcoholics must face when they disclose their sobriety experiences. Since public speaking is a common form of what AA calls "service work" women alcoholics open themselves to a kind of public vulnerability whenever they disclose their life journeys in public spaces. While the elders whose stories we have been considering entered sobriety at a time when there were few women in AA and, in fact, women are still in the minority in this fellowship, they still spoke with warmth about the experience of sobriety—despite its potential difficulties and pitfalls. How were they able to navigate this difficulty?

A FEMINIST PRESENCE

One piece of the puzzle falls into place when we consider writings in feminist theology. Feminist authors, both past and present, correctly caution that women's experiences have been excluded from theoretical models until very recently, and that this failure must be rectified if women are to be empowered.[1] Christie Cozad Neuger in *Counseling Women: A Narrative, Pastoral Approach* suggests a model for pastoral counseling that refashions therapeutic methodologies so that they are inclusive of women's experience, voice, and view. Her suggested approach allows the woman's account of her experience to be received, honored, and supported. Neuger refers to this method of attending as "feminist listening."[2]

Neuger voices grave concern that traditional forms of alcoholism treatment, which focus on powerlessness and loss of control, lead to a dramatic loss of self-esteem rather than the healing of essential identity as suggested by Stephanie Brown.[3] We could conclude that the women who participated in this project have experienced the very situations Neuger warns against. Is there a dilemma in trying to reconcile feminist models of pastoral counseling with the traditional models of alcoholism treatment and recovery? Does the paradigm of powerlessness and unmanageability found in Alcoholics Anonymous inflict harm to women whose self-esteem is already dangerously low?

Elizabeth Johnson beautifully illustrates this dilemma in the classic text *She Who Is: The Mystery of God in Feminist Theological Discourse.* In this foundational work, Johnson provides an analysis of conversion, which as we examined in Chapter 2, is an essential element of the recovery process. Johnson examines Christian conversion from a feminist perspective and reminds us that conversion begins with decentering. Classical accounts of conversion focus on the person who is puffed up with pride and whose attention must be decentered, turned away from narcissistic self-involvement. But when the person suffers from a lack of pride, or to use more current language, shame and low self-esteem, then the point of conversion must speak to this unique experience. In this context then, to be converted means that the person is *restored to centeredness*.[4]

The problem, according to Johnson, is directly related to the two ways that power and powerlessness might be experienced. Power for those who have power can be an occasion of sin, to use more traditional language, and when abused requires a subjugation of self. For the powerless, a subjugation of self simply continues an already active diminishment of identity. Simply put, women are not inclined toward overblown egos and therapeutic strategies that focus on ego deflation and the "disowning" of self simply perpetrate a second victimization.[5] In this way of thinking, feminist and womanist therapeutic and theological models seem to be in direct conflict with Stephanie Brown's assertion that power and control are the central issue to be addressed by all people who enter the recovery process.

But perhaps this is only an apparent dichotomy. The critical element to keep before us is that women alcoholics act in destructive ways. They are dissimilar to women on the whole (who also may be struggling with dominant structures of power and control) in one key way: they act badly, destructively, cruelly, and willfully when drinking. And although they may have begun life as victims, their subsequent behavior belies that fact; indeed, it places it as a secondary concern. This is the terrible reality of women who have moved from ordinary time to extraordinary time; they have moved from concerns of the spirit so present in struggles for equality and parity to a place of spirit-death and shame. The literature on shame warns that to deny the reality of a person's lived experience is to further the experience of shame and isolation. What Neuger calls "feminist listening" seems to require that the pastoral counselor *hear a woman's story as she has experienced it,* bad and dangerous behavior included, and not as they would prefer to hear it.

FACING THE SHADOW

The women whose stories we have been considering believe that this is especially critical for women in early recovery. Newly sober women need to be supported in facing the facts of their drinking behavior and the consequences for those in relationship with them. To attempt to protect them from this act of taking responsibility is to treat them as less than whole, less than adult, less than human. An Alanon axiom states that it is disrespectful and cruel not to allow adults the simple human dignity of the consequences of their actions.

This does not resolve the conflict completely, however. Is confrontation necessary when it could be said that women suffer a double tragedy of loss of self and loss of self-esteem in a society that does not tolerate bad behaviors from women? Several of the women's stories offer a recasting of this dynamic. Perhaps most revealing are some of the accounts of confrontation of women by women. We can recall accounts given earlier: *NH tells of the woman in AA who sat at her feet and gently asked her why she drank. PJ tells of AA women who came to her home, washed her hair, and bathed her so that she could attend an AA meeting.* These are indeed confrontations, but not in the sense that feminist theologians have correctly warned us against, and therein lies the difference. When confrontations about drinking behavior happen within the context of loving concern, the damage seen in harsher confrontations is avoided, shame is not reinforced and repeated, and healing might begin.

This interpretation might help us to see how long-sober women are able to hold together the "yes" involved in letting go of pride and self-centeredness related to drinking behavior while also saying "yes" to new notions of self and of God; how they might say "no" to patriarchal notions of self and God and "no" to thoughtless and sexist behavior.[6] Women in recovery need to be assisted and supported in taking hold of despair and in redirecting it. The self-reclaiming process detailed in Chapter 2 does not prevent women from realistically reconsidering who they are in a decidedly fallen world, however, it does require walking a razor edge where fragile self-esteem is balanced by the need to face up to bad or sinful acts.

NO LONGER A STRANGER

As noted earlier, long-sober women are the first to remind us that they came to recovery at a time when women were treated as second class in virtually all aspects of life, necessitating this caution about harsh therapeutic strategies. How do long-sober women deal with the fact that they have lived their recovery within a fellowship that was constructed by men for men?

This is not a new issue; rather it is a situation that is all too familiar to Christian women who struggle to achieve equal status in the church. In *The Religious Imagination of American Women*, Mary Farrell Bednarowski writes about the ways in which women come to terms with religious traditions that are not entirely open to their voices and gifts—one method is the adoption of a perspective that views "ambivalence as a modern theological virtue."[7] She states:

> What I find particularly interesting is the fact that many women no longer look on the shaping power of religion as primarily insidious and therefore to be resisted, as was more typically the case earlier—as a product of the tools of the master, whose house can never be dismantled by those same tools. . . . The formative powers of religion are regarded as constituting a more dynamic reality with the capacity for both good and ill. By acknowledging their willingness to shape this formative power in ways that are transformative, women make it clear that they do not experience themselves at the mercy of their traditions but instead are responsible for them along with other members of their communities.[8]

Women in sobriety seem to share with their Christian sisters this openness to be formed by a spiritual tradition while reforming that same tradition through their own steady faithful presence.

This is one way to understand and interpret the mixed experiences of women elders in AA. Their experience within the AA tradition is painful, yet healing. AA has been home to them, despite the fact that their presence has not been reflected in literature and other expressions of the tradition until more recently. It was within this tradition that they experienced and learned to practice reconstructed versions of listening and confronting, a tradition that maintains its power to reconcile and heal. Moreover, the idea of "ambivalence as virtue" offers one solution to the dilemma posed by therapists and theologians alike: why do women stay in AA? One answer seems to be that they stay because they are responding to principles that express universals, *and which cannot be contaminated by the traditions that contain them.*

We can see this "piety of ambivalence" in the live narratives of long-sober women.[9] PK told the following story about her experience in a meeting attended predominately by men. She describes the change in spiritual sensibilities that take place in sobriety—for women and men alike:

> I went to AA and then I had two years where I didn't go because I couldn't find a meeting in Minneapolis, where we had moved to. Again, it was an amazing grace that I ever survived without it. . . . Part of it was that I was in a real dry drunk. So I was trying to make everything outside of me perfect because everything inside was really dying. I decided that I really had to find a meeting and stick with it. I went to an all-women's group and I didn't like it. I went to another group and didn't like it. About two Sundays later I went to church and after Mass we would get together and have coffee. This man I knew came up and we were talking and I told him that I was having a heck of a time finding a meeting—it just slipped out. And he said, "Hey, are you a friend of Bill W's?" He knew I lived nearby and he told me that his home group was in the neighborhood. [She chuckles.] He said, "Do you want to come? It's a lot of guys and we need some more women!" So I told him I would go. I knew him and liked him and I thought that he was safe.
>
> And I got into this group that was almost all guys and I thought, "Oh Lord!" [She laughs in delight.] I can say that from that day on—and I grew up with boys and so I was comfortable with men—but I thought that it wouldn't work. I kept coming up with all these reasons but I kept going back, you know. He was holding me accountable until I was done with six weeks. And they turned out to be the most nonjudgmental group of men that I have ever met in my life. You get them out of the room and some of them are knuckle-dragger machismos, but in that room is the leveling force that we are all alcoholics and they will do anything, anything to help you achieve that goal of being sober that day. I had never experienced that in any group before. I know that women have walked into the group just off the street, or have been referred to the group and they kind of reel. I tell them, "Just sit down. These guys are okay." I refer to God in the feminine and some of them just say, "Hmmmm." And some of them have started saying, "He or

She" for God. [She laughs.] I have a sponsor there who is a male, and that is something I have never done, but I also have a sponsor who is a woman, so there is balance there. So that group all of a sudden, kept me grounded and things have been wonderful since then. I am really grateful that I didn't have a slip in those years before.

This story resonates with Bednarowski's conceptual model, which suggests that in practicing the virtue of "living with," women can embrace a tradition and in so doing change it and make it their own.

ACTING AS IF

An active practice of the virtue of ambivalence requires a commitment from therapists and pastoral counselors as well. Counselors must resist the urge to "homogenize" the stories of woman in early recovery, must resist premature comfort and reconciliation. This willingness to live with and tolerate her discomfort will allow her story to be told more completely. Although it might be tempting to question the wisdom of a woman's decision to begin sobriety in AA, with all of its masculine and potentially sexist trappings, it is not always helpful to do so. The women elders to whom we have been listening remind us that women with long-term sobriety seem to have found a way to live within the reality of this flawed fellowship. They see the flaws and they have decided to live with them, to affect the fellowship from within. Their presence is a kind of resistance constructed out of presence or "being" that has the power to shape the fellowship from the inside out.

In *A Feminist Ethic of Risk*, Sharon Welch describes the characteristics of this kind of resistance. She describes feminist risk taking as being a new understanding of responsibility, an understanding that is "grounded" in a community of support, and a willingness to engage in calculated, deliberate actions without concern for a guarantee of success.[10] Thus, feminist risk taking is a kind of relational resistance, characterized by the willingness to "act as if," despite overwhelming evidence that individual action will have few observable outcomes. Welch writes, "Responsible action means changing what can be altered in the present even though a problem is not completely resolved. Responsible action provides partial resolutions and the inspiration and conditions for further partial resolutions by others. It is sustained and enabled by participation in a community of resistance."[11] This willingness to faithfully represent an alternative reality is precisely the willingness role modeled by the women elders in AA. Theirs is a steadfast presence that lights the path for women new to recovery.

Welch warns of the cynicism that sometimes emerges when those resisting (she is particularly interested in the moral agency of European-American women) are unable to realize the societal changes that are being sought. A temptation to control, asserts Welch, results in a loss of energy to continue to work for change.[12] Stephanie Brown also cites the temptation toward control. Indeed, she offers this rather harsh injunction to the therapist or pastoral minister who wishes to assist alcoholic clients: "As long as the therapist maintains a belief system based on the idea of self-control and the belief in the responsibility and power to make the alcoholic change, treatment for alcoholism will remain problematic.[13]

The serenity prayer, composed by Reinhold Niebuhr and popularized by AA is another expression of the principles at the heart of the ethic of risk. In its long form it reads:

God grant me the serenity
To accept the things I cannot change,
Courage to change the things I can,
And wisdom to know the difference.
Living one day at a time,
Enjoying one moment at a time,
Accepting hardship as the pathway to peace.
Taking, as He did, this sinful world as it is, not as I would have it.
Trusting that He will make all things right if I surrender to His will.
That I may be reasonably happy in this life,
And supremely happy with Him forever in the next.
Amen.[14]

Similarly the AA mandate to seek ways in which individual experience can benefit others comes to mind here. Certain "promises" are detailed in the sixth chapter of the Big Book. It reads:

If we are painstaking about this phase of our development, we will be amazed before we are half way through. We are going to know a new freedom and a new happiness. We will not regret the past nor wish to shut the door on it. We will comprehend the word serenity and we will know peace. No matter how far down the scale we have gone, we will see how our experience can benefit others. That feeling of uselessness and self-pity will disappear. We will lose interest in selfish things and gain interest in our fellows. Fear of people and of economic insecurity will leave us. We will intuitively know how to handle situations that used to baffle us. We will suddenly realize that God is doing for us what we could not do for ourselves. Are these extravagant promises? We think not. They are being fulfilled among us—sometimes quickly, sometimes slowly. They will always materialize if we work for them.[15]

In summary, it might be said that stories we have been considering illustrate one example of the "virtue of ambivalence" as practiced within a program of recovery that was not initially intended for those who are now practicing it.[16] Embracing and living out sobriety through such a model requires a reconstruction of how one confronts, supports, and relates to others. Finally, this virtue of ambivalence has to be practiced with the full recognition of the AA tradition, as it is, while understanding that long-term changes resulting from a multitude of individual acts may not be immediately apparent.

This pragmatic approach was echoed frequently in the narratives of long-sober alcoholic women. KP's account of her experience held what is perhaps the most succinct description of the steadfastness of long-sober women. She concluded her narrative with this wry comment about her longevity in the program: *My whole life is wrapped around AA. So that's my story and I am still alive and well. How you become an old-timer is you don't drink and you don't die.*

Chapter 7

To Speak Rightly of God

TUNING IN

The very first elder to agree to share her sobriety story was PH. She had celebrated thirty-five years of sobriety at the time of our interview and offered the following "what happened" account detailing her first moments of sobriety.

Finally, one night I woke up—and I had lived in this house for fourteen years—and instead of turning right to go to the bathroom, I turned left and I pitched down the entire flight of stairs. If I hadn't been drunk I would have been killed. The stairs were carpeted but I had a rug burn on my foot. . . . And my husband said to me the next morning, "I don't care what you do but get an appointment with the doctor. You have to do something." There was a place started by a Catholic priest and it was one of the first treatment centers in the country. I had read an article about Antabuse [a prescribed drug that causes drinkers severe discomfort] and I thought, "Well, I can call this place and they can give me these pills and then I won't ever have to drink again." And that's how mixed up and crazy I was. I called and the secretary convinced me to call AA; and that's what I did. I am one of those lucky people that from my very first meeting—that was October 24, 1966—I have never to this day taken another drink. That's the real miracle. And all it took was that first meeting and I knew the answer was there. I've never forgotten that meeting. The woman that spoke was a periodic drinker. I was hung over and belligerent and thought, "Well, she doesn't have a problem! If I could go six months without drinking I wouldn't have a problem. My problem is I can't go a single day without drinking." But there was enough of a glimmer there to bring me back to another meeting. My husband had it in his mind that I should go into a psychiatric clinic and thank God that I didn't because I am sure that I would have gotten on some kind of pills or something because really, in 1966 psychiatric facilities weren't doing a good job with alcoholics. And that certainly was God acting in my life.

Rising from the Dead
© 2007 by The Haworth Press, Inc. All rights reserved.
doi:10.1300/5800_07

What's going on here? For PH God's grace is clearly present in her suffering and in her awakening. She sees God acting in her life, inviting her to a new life.

What's going on here? This is the question posed by those who suffer and answered by those who believe. In my years of teaching introductory classes in theology I have learned that it is helpful to begin with this elementary question and in my time with long-sober alcoholic women I have learned that the answer can be both surprising and powerful. In its essence, lived spirituality is an answer to the question, "What is going on here?" The various world religions offer responses to this question of meaning, providing answers about the significance of events, experiences, and situations. We receive a telephone call at just the right moment, or a person crosses our path at just the right time, a friend says exactly what we need to hear. What is going on here? Our answer to this question reveals our basic orientation to life's most elemental questions, such as our understanding of God, of self, and of suffering.

Long-sober women live out of a rich understanding of the dynamic, creative action of God in the world. The stories I collected are literally peppered with reference to the ways God takes direct action in ordinary lives lived in ordinary time. An intense familiarity with God abounds in these life stories—these are women who are fully engaged in a relationship with God. Their answer? God is absolutely concerned with their daily experiences and efforts and absolutely active in the unfolding of their lives and destinies. This God reconciles the distance between human and Divine, and takes our cares and worries personally. God is seen as active in persons and in relationships. God puts people in the path so that encounter might take place, or God softens the heart of the speaker, or God softens the heart of the listener. In each case, God is seen as an active agent, intervening on behalf of the woman in need.

Women new to sobriety are taught to seek, through prayer and meditation, knowledge of God's will for them (step eleven). The result is a life of "spiritual attention" that results in a spiritual awakening (step twelve). This conscious contact with God causes a dramatic change in the interior life of the person. One of the fruits of this dynamic spirituality is the recognition of God's grace within the terrible experience of alcoholism. God is seen as a consistent loving presence whose grace ultimately unifies the shattered self. Recounting the story of her last drunk, KP gave this account of God's reconciling presence.

> *I set about to drink myself to death.* I drank straight for about six weeks. I never ate when I drank because I didn't want to put the fire out, and besides, when I would sober up I couldn't eat so I would have to have another drink just to keep going. And by this time I was just wanting oblivion—not to feel, not to think, not to even be there. And when I ran out of booze and money, then I had to sober up. And that was when I was so miserable, and so desperate, and so in despair; twenty-three years old and just in despair. That was when I asked God for help. And surprise, surprise, He answered my prayers. He gave me such a peaceful feeling, so much serenity that I never knew in my life. And I knew that there was a God and that He did love me and that I was going to be okay. Later that afternoon, this lady that I knew in AA . . . I could hear her voice out in the hallway. I thought, "Oh God, I'm hearing things again." And why would I think of her, why would I think it was her out there talking to the bellhop. So I called down to the desk and asked if she lived there. I asked them to ring her room and they said that she was moving into the room right next door to me! God works in wonderful ways! And I talked to her and told her what had happened to me and about this feeling I had had and everything. She dropped everything and came over. She talked to me—I was so weak from not eating for so long. She fed me and she stayed with me all night. Now for someone to put themselves out so much for someone like me, who didn't deserve to be treated as well as she was treating me. That's what I felt about myself. I had done so many terrible things, how could anybody want to help me? You know you get that old guilt feeling. We're harder on ourselves than anybody else could ever be. But she did that for two or three days until I could go downstairs by myself and get my own meals. And we became very, very close. In fact we even had an apartment together after I went back to work. I had lost my clothes hither and yon, I had lost my shoes hither and yon; I had one pair of shoes but they weren't mates! I had a left and a right but they weren't mates! So I had to go back to work in order to get some clothes and just start living my life again—my brand new life, not the one I had!

This is a heart-wrenching story yet KP related it with a quiet peace. KP's story holds an image of God that is resonant and rich. Imagine saying the words, "I set out to drink myself to death" and then following these words with a story of redemption! The power in this story rests on the image of God contained within it; this is an experience of Divine sympathy and sorrow. This is a God who regrets the pain of self-inflicted shame. In KP's story of hitting bottom we see an amazing intersection of people and experiences. At the very moment she asks God for help she hears the voice of someone in the sober community, someone she knows. This helper moves into the space that KP inhabits—the place of shame and despair—and KP is healed. She is now able to begin living her "brand new life." She has been brought back from the brink.

IMAGINING GOD

A return to Elizabeth Johnson's work will assist us in breaking open the image of God contained in KP's redemption story. Johnson suggests a richly textured account of what it means to "rightly speak about God."[1] Correct language about God must include an acknowledgement of two things: the complexity of human experience, both male and female, and the ways in which growth of the self affects growth in knowledge of God. Language about God must be grounded in tradition and yet remain open to new forms and insights. Johnson is particularly interested in God's sympathetic interest in those who suffer and suggests that classical theological models do not do full justice to the God of infinite sympathy. The lives of women suffering with addiction provide one example of this image of God's sympathetic interest. Long-sober alcoholic women live out of a new image of God active in their lives. In this new understanding of God, the entirety of life is given new meaning; past, present, and future are held together by the grace and light of God's love. Situations that might have seemed pathetic and tragic take on new significance. They are now included in a coherent story—a redemption story in which every moment contains the capacity to communicate about God's reconciling love.

FB told the following story about her life before sobriety. Her sense of shame and isolation is poignantly clear, yet FB is also intensely aware of God's presence in her life.

> My husband and I drank a lot and he was abusive. We were married nineteen years and my alcoholism got progressively worse. I had affairs because I wanted to be around somebody who was nice to me. I stayed the nineteen years but I never told anybody about the abuse. At this point my alcoholism had progressed to the point where I was hospitalized in a mental hospital for depression—but it wasn't depression. But nobody knew. And that is when I started using Valium. They gave it to women for "nerves." And my life was going down very fast during

those years. I had been active in politics, I was chair of the children's symphony, I was president of the church women. I had found in myself that I had some gifts. But when that pattern started I had to give up one thing and then another. I couldn't come through. I started living a lie. And that's when the lying really started.

And in the divorce I moved back to my hometown and nobody really watched me and my drinking. And that's when I really started to go down. I was thirty-nine years old and I was drinking probably a fifth of scotch a day. And I was passing out—going to bed and passing out. And I had these two precious daughters. Trying to get up and be their mother, trying to get up and drive them to school and shaking so bad. I set the alarm so I could get them to school. My friends were drinking too. And they all had problems. But I just had so many blackouts and my behavior was so shameful it was almost like I hated myself so much. It is hard to describe that kind of thing. I was trying to live up to here [she holds her hand up high] and I was here [she holds her hand low] if that makes sense. I was trying to live up to what people thought of me. *And God works in this; I can see that now.*

Clearly FB sees God working in her life despite the shame and guilt. How can this be? This is an image of God in relationship with women, that they might draw strength from God's closeness as they walk that razor edge balancing self-esteem and self-responsibility. Elizabeth Johnson asserts that our idea of God must include the realization that while God may "permit" suffering, God is not unaffected by the pathos of a life of pain. For Johnson, "The connected self, typical of women's way of being in the world demands a different concept of God in the midst of suffering."[2] Undoubtedly FB experiences God as a companion in her suffering. She is never really alone in the wilderness of her drinking; God is her companion. This is a complex image of God is one in which the distance between Creator and creature is diminished through God's reconciling grace. In a metaphor particularly fitting for alcoholic women, Johnson writes, "Holy Wisdom does not abhor the reality of women *but identifies with the pain and violence that women experience on the cross, of whatever sort*" [italics added].[3]

While she would not label them as such, FB is painfully aware of the "crucifixion" experiences of women alcoholics. She is also keenly aware of the need for relationship as a vehicle for healing, both in her own life and in the life of others. This is FB's account of her first months in sobriety.

And when I was in treatment they had us do a fifth step. Even though I was only a little bit sober I went ahead and did it. I had to get rid of some of that stuff! So I asked this woman; I asked could that woman hear my fifth step? And that is when I got rid of all that shame I had been carrying around. And her reaction to some of what I said was, "Did you do that only one time? I did that five or six times!" [She laughs.] And I started to feel relief.

I chose a sponsor who was old enough to be my mother and she took that time. And people started to believe in me and see things that I couldn't see. And she had me very involved. I went on twelve-step calls. And my life, my world started bringing me into contact with people I would never in any way had any contact with. I was so isolated in this snobbish social world I had been brought up in. And it was never me and I knew that. And going on twelve-step calls where there were women who were lying in their own pee. And I did that. And the real me started to come out—like the velveteen rabbit in the story. I started taking meetings to the prison, to maximum-security prisons, state prisons where women had been in a blackout and murdered someone. I could see myself; I had so much hate toward my first husband I used to wish he was dead. And I started connecting with people. And love really poured out toward me. God brought me these people. My world started to change and I found myself connecting and connecting and connecting with these women.

A BRAND-NEW LIFE

Of particular interest here is the way that the various storytellers describe life experiences that illustrate the complexities of sin and deliverance. Feminist pastoral theology can seem to be focused on the vulnerability of women who have been victimized, yet the life narratives of long-sober women reveal an experience of victimization that is much more complex and multifaceted. The women I interviewed had to come to terms with the fact that they were both *victim and victimizer.* Coming to terms with such awareness demands a lived spirituality that can sustain the person as she traverses this terrible soul territory. Realization of one's own capacity to oppress can be deeply traumatic and shameful. Yet long-sober women have found a way to heal the guilt and shame that is incurred through actions that are truly harmful and hurtful. They have come to terms with what it means to behave as victimizers. They communicate this knowledge through redeemed life narratives and their life stories are full of images of God suffering as they engaged in tragic and damaging behaviors.

This complex self-awareness requires a deep sense of God's healing, reconciling presence, as found in AG's story about God's healing
presence within her tragic life choices.

> I began to look at my world around me and thought, "Why can't I stop?"
> I didn't care about my body, about myself. But a guy I knew helped me
> get into a methadone program. If he was going to help me then I had to
> try it his way. So I did. And I had an apartment and my life was stable
> and I started working there but I still had a connection with my old life.
> So at the end of the day I started to do some hustling to make ends
> meet. And they would take the money and buy dope and I would use it
> to pay bills but one day I said, "You know what, give me some of that."
> And I know this was God because they just gave me water and told me
> that I wouldn't feel anything because of the methadone. This guy that
> had helped me told me that I needed to come through for him and not
> mess up and so I got on my knees that night and said, "Lord, if you let
> me keep this job I will never ever try anything else." And from that day
> to this day I have never stuck a needle in my arm. Now, back then—
> thirty some years ago—you didn't have to stop drinking. Okay, you
> could drink; that was legal! So there I was on methadone and we'd
> have parties for the clients and we'd go to these big garbage cans and
> just pour fifths after fifths of different alcohol and put some punch over
> it. And counselors could be drunk as a skunk and it was no big thing.
>
> And you know, I had been walking down the street one day and I
> said, "Lord, I can't stop using alcohol. It's either I'm going to die this
> way or you are going to stop me. I gave up. I gave up at that point and
> thought, "I'm either going to go full throttle at it or He is going to stop
> me." Six years later some client was in my office and asked me, "How
> did you do it?" And I hadn't thought about it before that but it was God.
> Not me. Because I had been in all those treatment programs and I had
> been clean for six or seven months but would get a craving and get
> right back at it.

AG tells this story as a redeemed narrative, that is, she sees her life
in a new way as a result of a spiritual point of view. This is her brand-
new life, in which even the pain of addiction holds an image of God's
attention and grace. This new worldview is evident in virtually all of
the life stories shared by long-sober women. They contain deeply
painful accounts in which the narrator is "broken" by the catastrophic
nature of her actions while drinking, yet the brokenness is not the final chapter. All of the life stories we have considered include a shift in
emphasis from the tragic to the joyous, and this shift in perspective
grows out of the practice of spiritual attention seen in twelve-step
spirituality.

We considered the image of God who suffers as we suffer, a God who remains in relationship with those who suffer. Within this relationship, a change is made in us. These stories contain the seeds of change for the community as well as the individual. The real power of recovery narratives is their communal effect. They are redemption narratives and as such hold the power to heal both storyteller and listener. We turn now to the ways that these new stories reshape the communities that contain them.

Chapter 8

Radical Brokenness
and Radical Relationship

HEALING EXPERIENCE

Visitors and newcomers to AA are often puzzled by the laughter; laughter is a constant element of AA meetings. We have the expectation that recovery stories are serious business and the shame highlighted in accounts of "how it was" certainly adds credence to this expectation. The stories here illustrate how shattering life events transformed ordinary time into extraordinary time. The storytellers share how they were driven into that terrible place of shame and regret that holds the power to maim both body and soul, yet their accounts were full of laughter and hope. I have included notation of those glorious moments when one or another of the women laughed in delight at the absurdity of her assumptions and behaviors when drinking. They are noteworthy because they are so unexpected within the context of the horrid details being reported and they are evidence of how much the teller has been healed.

KA's account of her last drunk is a classic example of this paradox. She had fifty-three years of sobriety at the time of this telling.

> Anyway, this particular drunk, my last drunk—we remember the first drink and the last drunk. I lived out on ten acres and had a lot of animals. The reason I lived out on ten acres is because I thought if I went back to the farm, I'd be all right. So we got a farm. I had these two young hogs that were going to have piglets and my husband's dad came over to have lunch as he did often. And he brought over some beer. So I had a beer for lunch—and this was typical of how I ended up drunk. I had no thought of drinking. I certainly had not thought, "I'm going off and have a drunk today." He left and then I realized that my hogs were having pigs and I called my vet. And then, of course, I say, "I'd

better run and get some beer because I need to have some for the veterinarian. He was obviously a drunk too because he had a chauffeur drive him, probably had lost his license. He was addicted to drink like me so I went to the store and got the beer—got plenty—and of course we have got to have beer because it is a hot day. Well of course, the day went on and I got drunker and drunker and drunker. I went down into the pasture to see how the pigs were. And she started chasing me and so I jumped over the fence and we were irrigating because we had an orange grove. I jumped over the fence and fell in the ditch. And so then I went to the house and now my husband would be coming home and I have got to get cleaned up because I'm muddy and I'm drunk. So I went into my little bathroom to get cleaned up before my husband comes home and I fell down and hit my nose on the basin and then landed on the floor. And for the first time I couldn't get up. I'm so drunk that I just couldn't get on my feet. So I crawled to the bed and got in the bed and that's where I was when my husband found me. He was frightened at first then he realized I was drunk! [She chuckles.] And I don't know if I was so drunk that he just left me alone but the next thing I know, I wake up and I am in bed with blood all over my face and in my eyes. And that was my last drunk.

What the reader does not see in this account is the serenity in her face as she told the story. She sat with her hands folded in her lap and offered the account in rich detail, punctuating the more awful details with a smile and once a full belly laugh. How might the difference between her affect and her story be understood?

For a fuller understanding we must return to the principles examined in Part II. Stephanie Brown's account of the stages of recovery highlight the importance of ritual in marking milestones in sobriety. These milestones are grounded by concrete representations of the transcendent reality that is being named and honored. The newcomer to AA begins to both see and experience a change in essential self through a rethinking of life narrative. The concrete symbol of this change serves as a tangible sign of the change, and the sign makes the experience more real—something important has happened— something true and deep and everlasting.[1] A commitment has been made—a covenant forged out of the wreckage of a human life that is held in God's abiding love.

We might view this experience through the lens of sacramentality and the sacramental principle. This is my approach, in part, because I am Roman Catholic. Celebrating the presence of God through ritual and symbol is an essential feature of Roman Catholicism. It is rooted in our belief that God is revealed in and through created reality. It is what we do; it is who we are. And features of the sacramental principle do seem to be operative in the process of recovery. We can see hints of the sacramental action of God in the life narratives we have been considering.

SACRED EXPERIENCE

What is the principle of sacramentality? Roman Catholic theologians such as Richard McBrien define sacrament as "a reality imbued with the hidden presence of God."[2] McBrien reminds us that a "sacramental perspective" is one that sees the divine within the ordinary.[3] In this dynamic interplay between heaven and earth, God and person, ordinary life is transformed through participation in the extraordinary. This is the sacred reality made real in sacramental encounters. When long-sober women tell their stories, when they live out of the mandate to put their lives and life stories in service to those who still suffer, a bit of the light and fire of the Holy Spirit is present. The point of contact is a sacrament. Says McBrien, "The dichotomy between nature and grace is eliminated."[4]

But can the relational activity of the women we have come to know rightfully be called sacramental activity? Certainly this is an expansion of the very traditional categories of sacrament and sacramental action, yet as we have seen in Chapter 6, we must be willing to continuously stretch and pull at these traditional categories. The relational activity of long-sober alcoholic women offers a rich example of this incarnated, symbolic living out of the reconciling presence of God.

THE BODY OF CHRIST

The women in this study exemplify transformed lives, but can the relatedness that they model make any claim to a sacramental reality without direct reference to Christ? This would seem to pose a certain dilemma, since none of the participants made this claim and it is certainly not a claim that AA makes. Some who practice pastoral ministry and pastoral counseling will require a direct and clear link between God's saving action as revealed in Christ, and the related sacramental forms and actions. Echoing this issue, theologian George

S. Worgul warns, "Any sacramental theology that does not see Christ as the center of sacramentology is judged inadequate."[5] How might we build a bridge between these symbolic categories?

As noted earlier, the women storytellers did not identify their religious affiliations. They seem to be practicing sacramental spirituality that is self-consciously distant from the "center" of religion. Theirs is a sacramentality practiced between psychology and religion, between organized religion and organized therapy. Yet, as a Christian, I see hints of the Christ presence within the stories we are experiencing. Some traditional metaphorical categories seem to be a good fit with the spiritual practice of the twelve-steps. In the book *Memories of God* theologian Roberta Bondi provides a rich illustration of the light of Christ that seems a mirror image of these sobriety stories.

> Dorotheos of Gaza, a sixth-century teacher, once preached a sermon for the monks in his monastery who were grumbling that they had to put up with one another's ordinary, irritating presence. No, Dorotheos told them, they were wrong. He asked them to visualize the world as a great circle whose center is God, and upon whose circumference lie human lives. "Imagine now," he asked them, "that there are straight lines connecting from the outside of the circle all human lives to God at the center. Can't you see that there is no way to move toward God without drawing closer to other people, and no way to approach other people without coming nearer to God?
>
> There is something implied in the very shape of his imagined chart, however, that Dorotheos did not draw to the attention of his listeners—*that in the movement toward love, whether of God, or of another human being, there is an open space so close to the center of reality, that the human and the divine loves become indistinguishable. This, I believe, is the place of the Incarnation into which are gathered all the saints . . . and all who make up the body of Christ, and into this place we are all drawn by love, both human and God's. In this place the fixed boundaries of time are overcome. There we may converse with and be blessed by the saints. There we are taught and blessed by the dead as easily as by the living, and our wounds are healed as we traverse what once seemed to be the fixed boundaries even of our past* [italics added].[6]

The experience of long-sober women exemplifies one example of the dynamic experience of radical brokenness and radical relationship: as we draw close to one another for healing and love, we draw closer to God and, as Christians would describe it, to the Christ experience. Bondi's extrapolation of the theology of Dorotheos of Gaza offers a rich rethinking of the presence of Christ in loving, reconciling actions. AA, when examined in its real essence, can be understood as one kind of sacramental encounter that brings about elemental changes such as those seen in the collected stories. It could be said that in the process of being broken in a radical way, the women in this study were *remade with the capacity to enter a new life.* This remaking is constituted by daily and weekly spiritual practices whereby the person reconceives the meaning and purpose of life. A new life is crafted out of the wreckage of the past.

We must consider an important point here. This construction of a narrative, over time, and anchored by or expressed in concrete forms and symbols is essentially the same activity as that seen in communities of faith. The healing experience of life made new makes room, as it were, for women to come to terms with the decidedly imperfect actions of those in the program who would not honor their presence. AA would refer to this as focusing on principles versus particular personalities.[7] Theologian C. S. Song offers an account of what this kind of experience would require.

> A theology . . . that does not address itself to a living human situation remains a theoretical theology. It is a classroom theology, a theology of the lecture hall. This kind of theology may delight the head, but it neither pinches the soul nor pricks the heart. It is a theology that does not draw blood. . . .[8]

Long-sober alcoholic women in AA certainly live out of a kind of theological life template that draws blood—anything less would fail to speak to the depth of their experience.

The classical definition of theology is faith seeking understanding—central to this idea is that individuals seek to express, understand, integrate that which they hold to be most true, most essential, most real about creation. Long-sober women in AA model a language of meaning, a language of spirituality, a language of Divine sympathy because without it they would lose their moorings. No one can spend the amount of time that they have in the valleys without a sacred container to hold all that they have witnessed. Huston Smith writes that the world's religions are essentially in agreement about three things: what we should do, what we should be, and what we should see.[9] We should *do* ethics; we should avoid certain behaviors such as lying, cheating, stealing, murder, and adultery. We should *be* virtuous, meaning we should practice humility, charity, and veracity. And we should *see* a vision of a creation that is more complete, more perfect, and better than it ever appears from our small limited vantage point.[10]

The net result is that long-sober women are remade in such a way that they have the capacity to enter healing relationships with those who follow. They do this because it is what has been done for them. Participants consistently cited this theme—to put one's life narrative in service to another is the primary focus of a life of recovery. They would insist that this actually becomes an intuitive process: "we will intuitively know how our experience can benefit others."[11] They have developed the capacity for a deep relatedness that can absorb and heal the injuries of shame so painful to new members. They are able to model methods of confrontation that do not further the injury already done by drinking. They freely offer the hope found in laughter and a profound appreciation for the absurdities of life, and they never take the blessing of new life for granted. These are some of the fruits of radical brokenness transformed through sacramental action into the capacity for radical relatedness.

I offer the following story as an illustration. This conversation took place after the interview with PJ and KP was finished. I was accompanied to this interview by one of my contacts within the AA community. She was invited by PJ and KP to sit in on their interviews. In the following excerpt they discuss a woman who has returned to drinking. This is their account of the unnamed woman's experience and their discussion about how to bring her back.

> This friend of ours was sober six months and her teenage son shot himself. He and this girl had had an argument and he shot himself. But she did not drink. She only had six months of sobriety and she did not drink. I really took my hat off to her. And then at the same time, her other son was found murdered and it was a drug deal gone bad. They beat him to make sure he was dead. They shot him first.
>
>   But we are pretty sure she is drinking now. Her husband left her for a younger woman. Imagine losing two children in such violent ways. She still has one left. I called her awhile back and the man that she had been living with—I called her on a Monday—he had gone and killed

himself. And I called her that day and she said, "Oh KP, how did you know to call?" But I had called for another reason. And then she told me that he had just killed himself. I said, "Oh my God, when does it end?" She started drinking after the second son died. But that wasn't what threw her. What threw her was that right after that, her husband told her he wanted a divorce for this younger woman. That was the breaking point.

I note this story for the reader because it is an "ordinary" one. Stories like these are held within the sacred container crafted by women elders in AA. This story is not too horrible or too heavy to be held and healed by women elders in AA. In fact, the radically transformed life seems to be uniquely suited to receiving stories such as these—the deep pain can be taken on, taken in, and held as holy. A capacity to respond to the call to radical relationship is created.

And, while their presence offers such a healing in the world, long-sober women are rather like shadows in our communities—they give and heal and make the presence of God manifest without ever really calling attention to themselves. As the women in this project said to me, it is more important to be present to someone's suffering than to call attention to how you have performed this act, yet their healing actions are felt in the communities in which they reside. Researcher Maureen Sagot makes this same observation about women elders in AA.

> Who are these women? They may be our mothers, our sisters, our friends, our neighbors. They are the silent strong women who carry the wisdom and the memories of a healing process that took place despite the barriers to recovery. Addicted women today are waiting to hear their stories.[12]

We must begin to see the presence of long-sober women as a sacramental presence—they are like living sacraments expressing love and support and God's healing grace through their faithfulness to those who still suffer. They have risen from the dead and now walk among us.

Chapter 9

On the Road to Emmaus

TO BE RECONCILED

Recently I attended a conference on the subject of pastoral counseling practices for the elderly. A guest speaker, a professor of pastoral counseling, described in detail his dismay at encountering at a hospital bedside the family of a cancer patient, all of whom regularly attended twelve-step meetings but never attended church services. They allowed that, while they would appreciate his presence in prayer, they had trouble with talk of God and preferred the term "Higher Power." He told those of us assembled that he found praying to "the Higher Power" to be very disturbing and he warned us about falling into this kind of trap, all the while bemoaning the loss of faith that led to language like that requested by this particular family.

This story might call to mind the experience of the disciples after the crucifixion of Jesus. In Luke's Gospel we hear that the women go to the tomb but it is empty and two radiant men tell them not to look for the living among the dead. The women go and tell the others but they are not believed because their account sounds so preposterous. Not long after, two of the men travel to Emmaus, a village near Jerusalem. A stranger joins them and it takes them the entire walk and a shared meal before they recognize their companion to be the risen Jesus. Reflecting on their journey they exclaim, "Were not our hearts burning within us while he talked with us on the road and opened the Scriptures to us?" (Luke 24:1-35, NIV).

There can be a disconnect between pastoral ministers and the lived spirituality of those in long-term recovery. We might think of this as a wall or barrier between the world of recovery and the world of the church community—a wall where we might become too distracted to realize with whom we are walking. I became acutely aware of this

Rising from the Dead
© 2007 by The Haworth Press, Inc. All rights reserved.
doi:10.1300/5800_09

wall while conducting the interviews for this study. Since my doctor-
ate is in ministry, my perceived role as a leader in the Christian Church
was questioned a bit—and this was not without irony for me as a Roman Catholic laywoman! The storytellers wanted to know if I was ordained, if I was "religious," and if I meant to judge them. It should be
noted that I was saved from an even more extended exploration of my
affiliation with the church only because I had the necessary contacts
and referrals and because I speak the language of recovery with proficiency.

CRAFTING A COMMUNITY

In the process of collecting these stories I had bumped into the wall
of "difference" where trust had to be crafted with the greatest care.
Theologian Linda Vogel describes this experience as "standing at the
wall" and she believes that this is one of the critical features of religious education and formation.[1] I had to be willing to stand at the
wall and act as translator if I wanted to be given their sobriety stories.[2] Vogel describes religious education as a kind of embedded activity that takes place within the context of a faith community. It is a
cherishing and handing down of the sacred stories, making them new
to each generation. It is sustained and informed by the Spirit and by
actively embracing life's "dislocating events."[3] Vogel says that religious educators act as people who can speak "at the wall" and "behind the wall"; they are bilingual since they speak both within their
tradition and between traditions.[4]

Vogel's point is relevant to this discussion because it highlights
one role that pastors and pastoral counselors could take when dealing
with recovering people, who may enter sobriety with questions about
whether they have lost their place at the table, people whose AA
group might rent church space for meetings but never feel that they
are entirely at home in that space. The pastor's role could be that of
translator between ritual and symbolic experiences that may seem
dissimilar yet are similar in spirit and intention. The recovery community is a rich resource for pastors and pastoral counselors, albeit
one that seems to be misunderstood and often underutilized. As with
the recovering women in this study, the goal of the faithful Christian
is to be open to being reformed by God's grace. While the two might
use different vocabulary for this process, the process remains the

same. When religious educators such as the professor described previously categorize difference as alien, it is a loss of opportunity—and perhaps we could say that it is a loss of spirit.

Moreover, while the symbolic frame used by the women storytellers is not explicitly Christian, it is not so far removed from Christian sensibilities as to be unrecognizable. Robert Albers makes a clear case that religious communities have an important role in supporting and revisioning the person "shackled in shame."[5] In *Shame: A Faith Perspective* he describes the process through which a community of believers could become a community of hospitality and healing for those suffering from shame, and by inference, for those suffering from alcoholism. The process is straightforward:

> The Spirit's gift of community may be among the most under-utilized of all. This is due in part to the individualistic emphasis in our society as a whole . . . but it may also be due to the fact that true community is infrequently experienced in our contemporary religious institutions. Community is not something that can be fabricated or created by gimmicks. It needs to be appropriated as a gift that is given by the Spirit.[6]

This is of particular concern when members who suffer from the shame of alcoholism are women. Yet, Albers cites AA meetings as one example of dynamic communities that have the capacity to invite healing—something that the lives and experiences of the participants of this study have demonstrated.[7] A second illustration: during faculty meetings held in preparation for the beginning of the academic year a colleague and I were discussing our writing. When I described the interview process and the many poignant moments during my encounters with long-sober women she remarked, "Well, it will probably be good for these women to have their stories recorded. It will make them feel better about themselves that someone is interested in them." I was dismayed. Her response was both well intentioned and deeply disturbing. I found myself considering the commitment required when one embraces change such as that made by the women I interviewed. The change that is made in a person who would move out of the pale of ordinary time to be remade by the Spirit is both terrible and beautiful. My colleague's attempt at charity was misplaced. The women I interviewed possess an abiding strength of character— they do not need condescension, however well intentioned.

STANDING IN THE PRESENCE

The pastor or pastoral counselor who wants to counsel alcoholic women must be prepared to face brokenness that challenges the experience of living in ordinary time. As KP says, recovery is not for sissies. These are strong women, broken women, mended women—they have long histories of behaving in less than ladylike ways—and they are unapologetic in the classic sense of the term. They are more like the adulterous woman described in the Gospel of John than like the faithful companions Mary and Martha (John 8:3-11, 11:27-31). I suggest the adulterous woman (who is never given a name) rather than some of the better known women companions in Scripture because the adulterous woman's sin is made explicit, as is the communal judgment upon her, and it is precisely the characteristics of namelessness and shame that fit so well with the women in this study. In fact I overheard recently a woman with long-term sobriety tell a newcomer who was concerned about her past behavior, *"Don't worry, my dear. Remember, Jesus loved the bad girls best."*

This AA elder is modeling an approach to the Gospel that might be characterized as "full contact." Her attitude is reflected in the various narratives we have been considering. C. S. Song is right—this is a theology that draws blood![8] In fact, the various characters in the story of the adulterous woman offer an excellent example of the ways in which members of a faith community can become so interested in "being good" that they resist "being made good."[9]

Not long ago I was invited to give a Lenten reflection on the story of the adulterous woman. As I prepared my comments I realized that my affection for her grew out of my own childhood experiences of women caught in public behaving badly. This is an excerpt from my reflection:

> I must admit that I love a good story. This love of drama has been programmed into me by my family, which is full of characters and drama queens, alcoholic women who behaved badly and without regrets. My childhood was filled with women who wore bright red lipstick and nail polish and who lived fast lives. I found them to be beautiful and amazing and frightening; I had an aunt who went bankrupt as often as the law would allow, and while working her way toward her next great crash wore beautiful clothing and French perfume. You know, when I was a child and would hear the story of this woman and the Pharisees and Jesus, it used to really scare me. I knew this woman; she was one

of my relatives! I spent a good deal of my childhood afraid for the souls of these women I loved so much. Their lifestyles made them good targets. And I must admit that I have spent a good deal of my adult life intellectualizing my life experiences, missing out on the complexity and beauty revealed in these car-crash lives. My alcoholic family gave me an appreciation for chaos theory and French perfume. I have come to believe now, in middle age, that God loves a life lived out loud. I am no longer afraid for the souls of those wonderful wild women.

I want to focus on two elements of this story. They are (1) love of sneering and (2) rising above sneering. How do these themes work in this particular text? It is important to remember that there are several participants in this particular drama: the woman, a herd of men (Scribes and Pharisees) who are accusing her, and Jesus. Although Bible scholars warn against it, I find it compelling that there is a male/female dynamic here, a willingness to treat a woman as a kind of container for guilt and shame. This is the attitude that results in so much cruelty in the world today, toward women and men too. This is a dynamic of sneering; it is nasty and cruel and treats the woman as a means to an end—the end being catching Jesus in a breach of the law. The second element that I want to comment on is that Jesus does not engage in the power struggle. He does this by taking the conversation in a totally different direction—both mothers and therapists recognize this as redirecting negative energy and activity—Jesus channels the attention in a different direction. He is making a political move here— resisting the power constructs found in any institutionalized religion. In this way, then, we get a glimpse of Sacredness casting light into the shadowy reality that is institutionalized morality without any heart or soul or real-life face. Hierarchical power structures are of the world, and don't always lead us to a good place. The response Jesus offers to the Scribes and the Pharisees reveals the new territory possible if we are to take seriously the unique human face of all who come before us.

Let us turn our attention to the critical moment in the story of the adulterous woman—let us tune into the background hum of her shame and humiliation. I find it to be a difficult story. She is living in the world of right and wrong, good and bad—the world of clear boundaries between the nice people and the not-so-nice people. Just imagine how stunned she must have been when Jesus redirected the energy and focused in another direction. She is suddenly freed up to consider her real circumstance, unencumbered by the judgments of others. She stands before God without the toxic presence of her accusers and therefore is free to really consider the facts of her behavior and its consequences. A new place for her.

What is the lesson for us? Jesus' response to the adulterous woman can be seen as the paradigmatic response to shame and brokenness born of catastrophic acts. Jesus sits and listens, redirects, allows the healing space to be emptied of external judgment. This is a critical step if the goal is to accept full responsibility for sinful acts. This is a healing place where the individual can accept the guilt, but not the shame. This is the still place where the person begins to be remade. Through her own acts she has been broken, but now the healing can begin. And while secular formulations like those detailed in Part II may continue to describe the transition, a "what happened" stage as a puzzling experience with no easily quantifiable cause, women elders in AA are happy to remind you that it is God who enters a moment of ordinary time. In this process the ordinary is transformed so completely that the person is brought into and then continues to live life out of the paradox of ordinary time made sacred forever.

Radical relationship requires a deep commitment to the hope-in-action. It relies on a belief, to paraphrase Julian of Norwich, that all will be well despite evidence to the contrary. Women elders in AA reach out for those who are lost to drinking despite evidence that it is hopeless, and this action, this hoping-for is sacramentality in its essence. Radical relatedness—which is a kind of sacramental relatedness—holds together the hope for and possibility of change while remembering the sorrow of unhealed illness. It is a necessary acknowledgment that long-sober women live with. Remember that terrible account of the woman who lost everything including hope. In their response to her, the AA elders model the process of story crafting as saving work.[10] And in a re-formulation of this notion Marvin Shaw writes:

> We have not let go when we have merely responded to the call "Let go and I'll catch you!" It is not until we let go utterly, without outside guarantees, that we have gone beyond the point of demanding that reality be as we would like it to be.
>
> . . . Life is embedded in a larger sustaining whole, and yieldedness to this, participation within it, is the fulfillment of human existence; but we should add, this does not save us from our essential vulnerability. *Our trust should be in the experienced buoyancy of the water and not in any belief about why it must be so, or that no one ever drowns* [Italics added].[11]

What then do these stories have to offer the practitioner of pastoral care and counseling? Perhaps this one thing: there is a chasm between what Richard Rohr calls pastoral counseling for the "what, why, how of a person" and pastoral counseling for the "who."[12] Alcoholic women elders have deep insights into the way God invites us into sacred space, breaks us, and then returns us whole and beautifully mended with the *who* within us transformed. The difference then is the deep sacramental mystery of Spirit acting in the world independent of human agency and plan. Mystery can be encountered. It cannot be taught, learned, acquired, administered. We must always be humble before it and remember that the unfolding of the sacramental presence is always independent of our actions. Sacraments happen through the actions of God. We must watch for them.

Chapter 10

More Conversations in Ordinary Time

My experience with the women elders in AA has given me a new-found admiration for stories of every shape. I listen differently now. I learned from them how to really *pay attention,* and in some ways I feel as though I never really understood the process of listening before I met and listened to these amazing women. Now I find myself listening for the voice of God in many conversations.

Like others, I am in the habit of multitasking, listening while doing other things, making noises to indicate that I am listening but always splitting my attention between the storygiver and other myriad details. I found that with these stories I needed to pause over the details—to actually listen to each and every sentence to ensure that I got it right. In so doing I received a powerful lesson in how I hear in "ordinary time" versus hearing in extraordinary time. These stories opened me up and made me aware of the breath of God blowing through my own life. This was one of the unexpected gifts of their sobriety stories; they taught me about the power of listening one story, one sentence, one word at a time.

As I have shared these insights and interesting thing has occurred. Women whose lives have been reshaped by other catastrophic events have told me over and over again how much this type of narrative construction works for their experiences too. During a recent workshop a participant offered the following story: her cancer had been in remission for many years and had just recently returned. She had been told that her cancer was terminal. She said that the spiritual method of "telling a life," as practiced by alcoholic women, had given her an idea of how to tell her own life story. The details of the catastrophic event were different, yet the results were rather the same. Her life had been changed irrevocably by cancer and she could clearly see a "how it was, what happened, and how it is now" frame or structure in her

Rising from the Dead
© 2007 by The Haworth Press, Inc. All rights reserved.
doi:10.1300/5800_10

life. Her recognition of the relevance of twelve-step storymaking is not unique. Each life contains an arc of experience that includes pain and its companion, knowledge.

In this chapter we examine the power of attending to our own stories. What should we consider when constructing a life narrative and how might it relate to the narrative of the soul? How do these twin narratives shape our actions as members of the Body of Christ?

CONSTRUCTING A LIFE STORY AND A SOUL STORY

We get hints of the meaning of spirituality when we hear that twelve-step recovery is a program of living, that abstinence from addictive actions is only the tip of the iceberg, and that real recovery requires a program of spiritual growth. We understand that the twelve steps are a means of life reconstruction that lead to spiritual awakening. In fact, the twelfth step of AA reads, "Having had a spiritual awakening as the result of these steps we tried to carry the message to alcoholics and practice these principles in all our affairs."[1] We can see in the twelfth step one hint of a definition of spirituality. For those in recovery, spirituality is simply one's relationship with her Higher Power. Spirituality emerges out of the context of prayer and meditation. It is that simple. Women who enter recovery are yearning for something greater than themselves and in recovery they dedicate their lives to this search in all of their daily actions.

Although this discipline is not self-consciously inclusive of other life challenges, it has been applied widely to other kinds of spiritual journeys. We have only to look at the proliferation of twelve-step related fellowships such as Overeaters Anonymous, Gamblers Anonymous, and Emotions Anonymous for illustrations of the applicability of twelve-step spirituality to other life challenges. Which elements of the twelve-step path seem most applicable to the work of pastors, pastoral counselors and other helping professionals? How might the unique way that recovering people understand story be applied to others whose life narrative has become unraveled by trauma or loss? We will begin with the essentials of story construction in twelve-step practice—the spiritual autobiography.

WHAT IS A SPIRITUAL AUTOBIOGRAPHY?

Women who practice the twelve steps are familiar with the idea of documenting life story through the fourth and eighth steps. They know that to follow the spiritual path laid out in AA they must be searching and fearless about drinking behavior (step four) and about those whom they have harmed (step eight). They continue this focused self-examination in the tenth step, in which they maintain an awareness of everyday behaviors through regular personal inventory. In the eleventh step this awareness is deepened through prayer and meditation. This is at the heart of spiritual autobiography. A spiritual autobiography tracks the connections between life narrative and soul narrative; it connects the elements of one's life and holds them together. Simply put, a spiritual autobiography is a grand narrative or life story that encompasses both life story and soul story.

One way to approach the construction of such a story is to think of it as a combination of the insights and practices discovered through practicing the twelve steps. Together these experiences make up the lived spirituality that is practiced in the twelfth step. Because life stories and soul stories are dynamic, meaning that they change and grow as we change and grow, we can construct versions or models of spiritual autobiography yet the project is never completely finished. Like a map of the world, spiritual autobiography is a map of the inner world of the self. And, since it changes as we change and grow, it is always a view of conditions at present. The central questions addressed in spiritual autobiography are "who am I?" and "who is in charge?" The "who am I?" question concerns identity. What ideas are at the center of one's identity? The "who is in charge?" question addresses one's sense of powerlessness and control. When the answers to these questions become confused or mixed up, serenity will elude us.[2] We begin our journey with conditions at present.

Stories That Intersect: Conditions at Present

Journal Questions:

- Describe one experience from your childhood.
- What is memorable about this story? What does it tell you about your general beliefs about life, or about suffering, or about fate?

- Consider one of your close friends; perhaps this is a friend in recovery. Perhaps it is you life partner. Has this person told you
  stories? Which stories come to mind and why are they memorable?
- How do they relate to your story?
- How do they relate to what you generally think about life, or
  about suffering, or about fate?

Following the Steps—Walking the Labyrinth

Spiritual autobiography begins with a set of questions. These questions form the path we will take toward new insights and the new insights lead us to a new understanding of ourselves in the world. There
are many ways of thinking about this kind of journey. Often we envi-
sion our lives along a long straight line that stretches from birth to old
age. Other times our lives can feel like a huge spiral, with us spiraling
up or down as we are blasted by forces and pressures that seem too
much for us. And sometimes our lives just seem like a snarled rope
leaving us with no sense of direction or purpose.

I suggest that recovery is actually a journey through a great puzzle
or maze, like a labyrinth. Labyrinths are present everywhere. They
are found in the oldest human cultures and in modern structures and
landscapes. We see them set in the stone floors of medieval cathedrals
and mowed into the grass in gardens and parks. They seem to capture
in physical form our journey from question to insights to new sense of
self. When we apply the image of a labyrinth to our journey of recovery we see our life stories as journeys that circle inward and then out-
ward. Thus, the image of the labyrinth can serve as a path for charting
life stories and soul stories. However, I suggest one variation on the
classic labyrinth. We usually walk the labyrinth by entering at the
outside edge, walking in to the center, and then retracing our steps
back out. The variation I suggest is the beginning point. As we have
seen, the need to look inward often occurs during a crisis moment;
some event or experience or insight causes us to suddenly rethink
who we are and what meanings our life experiences reveal. This moment of sharp awareness is found at the center of the labyrinth.

LIFE AT THE LIMIT

Even though we tell our stories starting with how it was "before," followed by an account of what happened, and concluding with an account of how life is now, this is not how we actually experience the change, because our stories actually start with "what happened." They start with what psychologists and theologians call limit experiences.[3] Limit experiences are those occurrences that contain the seeds of transformation. They transform us by bringing us into a place that is between the old self and the new self. No one escapes limit experiences. They occur at every juncture of life, from the birth of a child to the death of a parent, from the loss of a job to the gain of a hard-won goal, from the first inkling of recovery to the realization that abstinence alone will not solve our problems. These limit experiences teach us about the boundaries of our ability to control—about what we can control and what we cannot control. They help us define and understand our limits. It is through this discovery that we might encounter the grace of community and the grace of God.

Beginning in the Middle: Limit Experiences

Journal Questions:

- Describe the experience that prompted you to consider your limits.
- What part of your life was interrupted by this event? Which relationships were disturbed by this event? Which goals were deferred due to this event?
- Identify the feelings you had during this experience.
- Identify five beliefs that were challenged by this event.

LIFESCAPE AND SOULSCAPE

What Is a Lifescape?

As we have seen, limit experiences can instigate a time of introspection. We begin to think about all of the decisions and events that lead up to this breakthrough moment. And, as our self-discovery continues, we begin to think about the path we will take following this breakthrough moment. The path leading toward the limit experience and the path leading away from the limit experience is the life landscape—lifescape.

Lifescape means simply the viewpoint or unique perspective of our lives. Life narratives are like landscapes; they reveal themselves in amazing ways.[4] Sometimes we can see all the way to the horizon, at other times we can see only as far as the top of the hill we are climbing. When constructing a spiritual autobiography we are often most aware of the hills and valleys of our everyday life experiences. Lifescapes tend to be populated with great characters, amazing scenery, and some very deep and frightening ravines. Once we have identified our beginning point—the limit experience that started our journey—then we can shift our focus and consider the events leading up to this moment. The experience of a limit is often accompanied by the realization that we have been thinking about ourselves in a certain way only to have this view challenged by the experience of powerlessness. Suddenly all of our assumptions about ourselves are called into question. We begin to reconsider life as we have come to know it. The second part of the lifescape is the realization that life can change. We can change. Our lifescape is supported by an accompanying set of beliefs and practices. The gift of twelve-step spirituality is that it frames this change experience within the context of a loving community and a commitment to putting one's life in service to others. In this way catastrophic experiences are transformed into grace-filled experiences.

What Is a Soulscape?

"Soulscape" means simply the landscape of our soul. It is the complex set of spiritual beliefs that accompany the lifescape. Soulscape is made up of our intuitions about a Higher Power, our struggles with powerlessness, and our beliefs about suffering. One way to think about soulscape is to think of it as a thread that is woven into the fabric of our lifescape, supporting it and deepening it. Limit experiences lead us to ask the difficult and deep questions such as, "What is my image of God? What is my understanding of the meaning of suffering?" As we practice the prayer and meditation suggested in twelve-step spiritual programs, our answers to these questions deepen. We see our lives transformed through the spiritual practices of the twelve steps. This complex interweaving of identity and attitude is our soulscape.

WALKING AND PRAYING A NEW LIFE JOURNEY

We have considered the three elements of spiritual autobiography: limit experience, lifescape, and soulscape. Now, using the image of the labyrinth, we will consider the details of this map of our spiritual selves. We began by standing in the middle and considering our limit experiences. Now we will contemplate the path we followed into the center and the path we wish to take out again. What are the characteristics of this path? This is the territory of lifescape and soulscape. From the vantage point of a limit experience we begin to reconsider and rewrite our life experiences and our deepest selves.[5] Now we are ready to consider how it was, and, how it is now. We do this by considering the various elements of lifescape and soulscape: pivotal moments, continuity, companions in the journey, obstacles, helpers, and lessons.

Pivotal Moments

Limit experiences lead us to revisit our life story and we often find that other crucial moments led to this breakthrough experience. As we consider our life landscapes from the vantage point of the middle of the labyrinth, we begin to identify these pivotal or critical events. These are the moments when the past and the future become illuminated by the bright light of a new idea or insight. We begin to see life in a new way and our sense of self seems to pivot, to turn us in new directions. Women in recovery often relate that working the third step is a pivotal moment, in which control is relinquished and the pretense of control is given up. Others describe the fourth step inventory as a pivotal moment in which they suddenly see patterns in their behaviors, attitudes, feelings, and actions. Pivotal moments are enriched by our soulscape experiences. Remember, these are the beliefs and hopes and prayers that occur at the deepest level of our awareness. They emerge out of our sense that God is working in our lives and, as the Big Book says, doing for us what we could not do for ourselves.

Pivotal Moments

These are crucial moments, crossroads moments that cast new light on the past and on the future. They light up the lifescape and soulscape.

Journal Questions:

Lifescape Questions

- Describe five pivotal moments leading up to your limit experience.
- Did they occur in childhood? Did they occur in adulthood? Were they peak or valley moments?

Walking out from the center to new life

- Describe five pivotal moments that you have experienced since beginning your path of self-discovery.
- Have they been peak or valley moments?

Soulscape Questions

- Identify some of the beliefs you believed to be true before beginning this new journey. Now identify the ways that these beliefs have been challenged.

Continuity

Every life has continuity. Continuity is simply all of the familiar experiences, places, people, and even ideas that make our lives feel ordinary. We cannot achieve a sense of security without continuity. One of the tragedies of addiction is the way that it causes the continuity of life to be disrupted and distorted. And addiction is not the only experience that can disrupt our experience of ordinary life. Unexpected illness, loss of employment, and divorce are only a few of the experiences that can disrupt our experience of the ordinariness of life, yet when we embrace this experience and confront the changes it has made in us, we find that we can begin to rebuild the continuity of our lives using different materials. Using our image of the labyrinth, we can look at our past to identify the elements that make up the continuity of what twelve-step spirituality calls "how it was." Then we can consider our lives as changed people and identify the elements that make up the stability and continuity of our new lives; this is the path to wholeness referred to in twelve-step spirituality as "how it is now." When considered together, these experiences suggest a fabric that holds our life story together. Continuity can include themes, scenarios, talents, beliefs, habits, and moods.

Continuity

These are the threads that hold together the woven fabric of our life story. They include themes, scenarios, talents, beliefs, habits and mood. What gives your life a sense of continuity?

Journal Questions:

Lifescape Questions

- Consider your life before.
- Describe five elements that gave your life a sense of continuity—and that you thought would never change. Were they attitudes? Specific beliefs? Emotions? Behaviors?
- Did they occur in childhood? Did they occur in adulthood?

Walking out from the center to new life

- Consider your life since. Describe how elements that gave your life continuity have changed.
- Does your life have a new kind of continuity? Describe the elements that give your life continuity now.

Soulscape Questions

- Identify how you might have answered the question, "Who am I?" before your limit experience.
- How has your answer to this question changed?

Companions in the Journey

Every one of us has companions in the journey. Sometimes these companions seem to be saints, other times they appear as sinners! The company of some can feel like a terrible burden while the company of others makes us feel whole and free. These characters populate our lives and travel with us. Like personalities in a play or movie, these characters move though out our lives, enlivening our lifescapes and soulscapes. One of the difficulties of addiction is the way that it distorts relationships. Addicts find themselves behaving in ways that can be frightening. Yet addiction is not the only experience that can change or distort relationships; however, the twelve-step model of narrative construction offers a way to reflect on difficult relationships and heal them. Finding the way back in relationships, healing relationships, is one of the gifts of twelve-step spirituality. When we consider our journey within the labyrinth, we begin to see patterns in our relationships, our companions in the journey.

Companions in the Journey

These are the great characters who populate our lifescape and who travel with us. They assist in holding together the woven fabric of our life story.

Journal Questions:

Lifescape Questions

- Consider your life before. Identify the characters that populated your childhood and adulthood.
- What were they like? How did they relate to you?
- Are your memories of them positive or negative? Did they make your journey easier? More difficult?

Walking out from the center to new life

- Consider your life since. Describe the characters that populate your new life.
- What are they like? How do they relate to you?
- Do they make your journey easier? More challenging? How many of the characters from your life before remain in your current life landscape?

Soulscape Questions

- Identify how you might have answered the question, "Who is God?" before beginning this new journey. How has your answer to this question changed?

Obstacles

It is not unusual to hear someone in recovery describe a difficult situation and then exclaim, "I am so grateful!" To those unfamiliar to twelve-step spirituality this can seem baffling. How can she be grateful for difficulty? How can she be grateful for a situation that should cause frustration, anger, and perhaps fear? The answer lies in the shift in attitude that takes place in recovery. The promises made in the Big Book remind us, "We will intuitively know how to handle people and situations that used to baffle us."[6] This new intuition comes as a direct result of working the steps. Yet it cannot be learned just by thinking about it; this is not an abstract lesson. We increase our ability to cope with difficulty by considering our experience through a fourth step inventory and by careful maintenance, as suggested in the tenth step daily inventory. At the same time we are invited to apply new insights when dealing with obstacles that stand in our path. No one has a barrier-free life. In recovery we learn to appreciate the very obstacles that used to frustrate us and rob us of our serenity.

Obstacles appear in many forms and can include people as well as situations. Sometimes our obstacles are internal, part of our self-talk, or our attitudes, or even our talents. When we consider our journey into and then out of the labyrinth, obstacles stand as roadblocks and then passages as we transform them from barriers to bridges.

Obstacles

These are the barriers we have encountered throughout our life journey. They can include attitudes, situations, people, talents, and intersections of events beyond our control. What obstacles have stood in your way or changed the path you followed?

Journal Questions:

Lifescape Questions

- Consider your life before. Identify five obstacles encountered in your childhood and five obstacles encountered in adulthood.
- Were the obstacles caused by an attitude? A situation or intersection of events? A person? Talents?

Walking out from the center to new life

- Consider your life since. Do you still encounter the obstacles you identified above?
- What new obstacles do you face? Are these new obstacles similar or different from the types of obstacles you faced in your life before recovery?

Soulscape Questions

- Identify how you might have answered the question, "Who is in charge of my life?" prior to your limit experience.
- How has your answer to this question changed?

Helpers

It is a truism that twelve-step spirituality cannot be worked in a vacuum. We are often reminded that the first word of the first step is "we." Indeed, all of the twelve steps are written in the plural. Change cannot happen without helpers; the more rigorous our path, the more we need the support of a beloved community. Helpers are those amazing spirit helpers who seem to make an appearance at just the right time. They seem to bring a message of promise at critical moments, shifting the balance from despair to hope. Each of us has that helping capacity. This dynamic causes people with long-term sobriety to tell the newcomer how needed they are. This can seem unbelievable to someone struggling in early sobriety, but it is so critical to the heart of twelve-step spirituality that it shows up in all aspects of the program. Thus helpers are found in that rich intersection of people, places, events, talents, and attitudes that we encounter along the labyrinth journey of our lives.

Helpers

These are the elements that seem to appear in our lives at the very moment that they are needed. Helpers can be people, places, events, attitudes, and talents. Who or what has unexpectedly arrived and helped you in your journey?

Journal Questions:

Lifescape Questions

- Consider your life before. Did you encounter helpers in your childhood? In your adult life?
- Were these helpers people? Were they places or events? Were they attitudes or talents?

Walking out from the center to new life

- Consider your life since. Identify the helpers that have appeared in your life most recently. Are these helpers people? Are they events or places? Are they talents?
- Identify any helpers that have stayed with you from the start of your journey.

Soulscape Questions

- Identify how you might have answered the question, "What is God's will for me?" prior to encountering a limit.
- How has your answer to this question changed?

Lessons

As we practice twelve-step spirituality we also grow in the wisdom that accompanies lessons learned, the final aspect of lifescape and soulscape that we will examine. In the AA community this same wisdom differentiates those who are "dry" and those who are "sober." Lessons require us to take personal responsibility and they foster self-awareness. This means having the willingness to know ourselves as we really are, not just as we wish to be.[7] Lessons in recovery become transparent through our practice of the prayer and meditation required by the eleventh step. Spiritual lessons are both earned and collected. They can be easy and difficult. As we have considered our path into the labyrinth and back out, we will have already identified some of the lessons learned. Some are carved into the terrain of our soul in painful and debilitating ways. When this is the case, lessons may move from the more neutral "lesson" category to the category of "obstacle." Lessons are best understood as ideas we live by. When we live out our lessons, we see the beginnings of the twelfth-step instruction to "practicing these principles in all our affairs."

Lessons

These are both earned and collected. They can be easy and difficult. Some are carved into the terrain of our souls in painful and debilitating ways. When this is the case, lessons may move from the more neutral "lesson" category to the category of "obstacle."

What lessons have you collected during your journey?

Journal Questions:

Lifescape Questions

- Consider your life before. Identify five lessons that you collected in childhood. Identify five lessons collected in adulthood.
- How many of these lessons came easy to you?
- How many were so difficult that you felt as though you had to earn them?

Walking out from the center to new life

- Consider your life since. Identify five new lessons that you have collected since encountering your limits.
- Have any of them come easily to you? Have any of them seemed difficult?
- How many of the life lessons you collected before have held true since?

Soulscape Questions

- Identify what you felt you had to offer the world prior to encountering your limit.
- How has your answer to this question changed?

WALKING INTO NEW LIFE

Practicing These Principles in All Our Affairs

The twelfth step reads, "Having had a spiritual awakening as the result of these steps, we tried to carry the message to alcoholics, and practice these principles in all our affairs."[8] After constructing our spiritual autobiographies we might well ask this question: How do we live into this new future we have been tracing in the pages of our journals? The twelve-step program of spiritual recovery gives us the answer: through service. The most striking and poignant feature of the stories of long-sober women was their great generosity and their concern that their stories offer some hope to women who still suffer.

The reason for telling spiritual stories is to ensure that others who suffer may be helped and healed. And amazingly, when we focus our attention on trying to be of service to others who suffer as we have, we too are healed. This is the elegant simplicity of twelve-step recovery. We could say that this is the Spirit of the God of our understanding acting as a healing presence in the world. The miracle of the twelve steps lies in witnessing the world being healed, one person at a time.

Appendix

THE TWELVE STEPS

1. We admitted we were powerless over alcohol—that our lives had become unmanageable.
2. Came to believe that a power greater than ourselves could restore us to sanity.
3. Made a decision to turn our will and our lives over to the care of God *as we understood Him.*
4. Made a searching and fearless moral inventory of ourselves.
5. Admitted to God, to ourselves, and to another human being the exact nature of our wrongs.
6. Were entirely ready to have God remove all these defects of character.
7. Humbly asked Him to remove our shortcomings.
8. Made a list of all persons we had harmed, and became willing to make amends to them all.
9. Made direct amends to such people wherever possible, except when to do so would injure them or others.
10. Continued to take personal inventory and when we were wrong, promptly admitted it.
11. Sought though prayer and meditation to improve our conscious contact with God *as we understood Him,* praying only for knowledge of His will for us and the power to carry that out.
12. Having had a spiritual awakening as the result of these steps, we tried to carry this message to alcoholics and to practice these principles in all our affairs.

Reprinted with permission of AA World Services, Inc.

Rising from the Dead
© 2007 by The Haworth Press, Inc. All rights reserved.
doi:10.1300/5800_11

THE TWELVE TRADITIONS

1. Our common welfare should come first; personal recovery depends upon AA unity.
2. For our group purpose there is but one ultimate authority—a loving God as He may express Himself in our group science. Our leaders are but trusted servants; they do not govern.
3. The only requirement for AA membership is a desire to stop drinking.
4. Each group should be autonomous except in matters affecting other groups or AA as a whole.
5. Each group has but one primary purpose—to carry its message to the alcoholic who still suffers.
6. An AA group ought never endorse, finance or lend the A.A. name to any related facility or outside enterprise, lest problems of money, property and prestige divert us from our primary purpose.
7. Every AA group ought to be fully self-supporting, declining outside contributions.
8. Alcoholics Anonymous should remain forever non-professional, but our service centers may employ special workers.
9. AA, as such, ought never be organized; but we may create service boards or committees directly responsible to those they serve.
10. Alcoholics Anonymous has no opinion on outside issues; hence the AA name ought never be drawn into public controversy.
11. Our public relations policy is based on attraction rather than promotion; we need always maintain personal anonymity at the level of press, radio and films.
12. Anonymity is the spiritual foundation of all our traditions, ever reminding us to place principles before personalities.

Reprinted with permission of AA World Services, Inc.

Notes

Chapter 1

1. Delores S. Williams, *Sisters in the Wilderness: The Challenge of Womanist God-Talk* (Maryknowll, NY: Orbis Books 1993), p. ix.

2. Delores S. Williams, *Sisters in the Wilderness*, p. xiii.

3. AA Services, *Alcoholics Anonymous; The Story of How Many Thousands of Men and Women Have Recovered from Alcoholism,* Fourth Edition (New York, Alcoholics Anonymous World Services Inc., 1955), p. 58.

The Twelve Steps and Twelve Traditions and a brief excerpt from the book, *Alcoholics Anonymous* are reprinted with permission of Alcoholics Anonymous World Services, Inc. (AAWS) Permission to reprint a brief excerpt from the book, *Alcoholics Anonymous* the Twelve Steps and Twelve Traditions does not mean that AAWS has reviewed or approved the contents of this publication, or that AAWS necessarily agrees with the views expressed herein. AA is a program of recovery from alcoholism *only*—use of the Twelve Steps and Twelve Traditions in connection with programs and activities which are patterned after AA, but which address other problems, or in any other non-AA context, does not imply otherwise.

4. AA Services, *Alcoholics Anonymous,* p. xiii. From the forward to the first edition, 1939.

5. Several books are key for understanding the program of recovery as suggested by Alcoholics Anonymous. The following titles are published by Alcoholics Anonymous World Services Inc., New York: *Alcoholics Anonymous,* Fourth Edition; *Twelve Steps and Twelve Traditions; AA Comes of Age; As Bill Sees It; Dr. Bob and the Good Oldtimers; Pass It On.*

6. Rebecca Chopp, *Saving Work* (Louisville, KY: Westminster John Knox Press, 1995), pp. 73-74.

7. From "Song of the Body of Christ" by David Haas, Copyright © 1989 by GIA Publications, Inc., 7404 S. Mason Ave., Chicago, IL 60638 www.giamusic.com 800.442.1358. All rights reserved. Used by permission.

Chapter 2

1. For a history of Alcoholics Anonymous see Ernest Kurtz, *Not-God: A History of Alcoholics Anonymous* (Center City, MN: Hazelden Educational Services, 1979) and Bill Pittman, *AA: The Way it Began* (Seattle: Glen Abbey Books, 1988). For a history of AA in Minnesota see Forrest Richeson, *"Courage to Change": Begin-*

nings, Growth and Influence of Alcoholics Anonymous in Minnesota (Minnesota: M & M Printing, 1978).

2. Carl E. Thune, Alcoholism and the archetypal past: A phenomenological perspective on Alcoholics Anonymous (*Journal of Studies on Alcohol* 38(1) 75-88, 1977), p. 79.

3. AA Services, *Alcoholics Anonymous; The Story of How Many Thousands of Men and Women Have Recovered from Alcoholism,* Fourth Edition (New York, Alcoholics Anonymous World Services Inc., 1955), p. 58.

4. Carl E. Thune, Alcoholism and the archetypal past, p. 80.

5. Ronald Takaki, *A Different Mirror: A History of Multicultural America.* (Boston: Back Bay Books, Little, Brown and Company, 1993), p. 15.

6. Barbara Anne Keely, Ed., *Faith of Our Foremothers* (Louisville, KY: Westminster John Knox Press, 1997), p. 47.

7. James L. Griffith and Melissa Elliott Griffith, *Encountering the Sacred in Psychotherapy: How to talk with People About their Spiritual Lives* (New York: The Guilford Press, 2002), p. 24. See also Richard Rohr, Liminal space: Days without answers in a narrow space. *National Catholic Reporter,* February 1, 2002 <natcath .com>.

Chapter 3

1. For a detailed history of the Minnesota model of alcoholism see William L. White, *Slaying the Dragon: The History of Addiction Treatment and Recovery in America* (Boulder, CO: Chestnut Health Systems, 1998).

2. Bromley Johnson, Former Director, Chemical Dependency Family Therapy Treatment Program, College of St. Catherine. Interview by author, November 25, 2005.

3. For an extensive discussion of the concepts of sacred and profane space, see Mircea Eliade, *The Sacred and the Profane: The Nature of Religion* (New York: Harcourt Brace Jovanovich, 1959).

4. This is especially true in classic alcoholism texts such as Vernon E. Johnson, *I'll Quit Tomorrow* (San Francisco: Harper & Row, 1973) and Philip L. Hanson, *Sick and Tired of Being Sick and Tired* (Minneapolis, MN: Park Printing, 1980).

5. Stephanie Brown, *Treating the Alcoholic: A Developmental Model of Recovery* (New York: John Wiley & Sons, 1985), p. 91.

6. Vernon E. Johnson, *I'll Quit Tomorrow* (San Francisco: Harper & Row, 1973), p. 27.

7. Ibid., pp. 35, 172.

8. AA Services, *Alcoholics Anonymous; The Story of How Many Thousands of Men and Women Have Recovered from Alcoholism,* Fourth Edition (New York, Alcoholics Anonymous World Services Inc., 1955), p. 82.

9. For a detailed analysis of congruence in addiction therapy see also Timmen L. Cermak, *Diagnosing and Treating Co-Dependence: A Guide for Professionals Who Work with Chemical Dependents, Their Spouses, and Children* (Center City, MN: Hazelden, 1998).

10. C. S. Lewis, *Mere Christianity* (New York: HarperCollins, 1952), p. 52.

11. Stephanie Brown, *Treating the Alcoholic,* p. 92; Vernon E. Johnson, *I'll Quit Tomorrow,* p. 31.

12. Mary Field Belenky, Blythe McVicker Clinchy, Nancy Rule Goldberger, and Jill Mattuck Tarule, *Women's Ways of Knowing* (New York: Basic Books, Inc., 1986), p. 3.

13. Stephanie Brown, *Treating the Alcoholic,* p. 105.

14. Ibid., p. 33.

15. AA Services, *Alcoholics Anonymous,* p. 58.

16. Vernon E. Johnson, *I'll Quit Tomorrow,* p. 49.

17. Stephanie Brown, *Treating the Alcoholic,* p. 106.

18. William James, *The Varieties of Religious Experience; A Study in Human Nature; Being the Gifford Lectures on Natural Religion Delivered at Edinburgh in 1901-1902* (New York: Modern Library, 1902), p. 414.

19. AA Services, *Alcoholics Anonymous,* p. 82.

20. Mary Field Belenky, Blythe McVicker Clinchy, Nancy Rule Goldberger, and Jill Mattuck Tarule, *Women's Ways of Knowing,* p. 3.

21. Stephanie Brown, *Treating the Alcoholic,* pp. 67, 138.

22. Ibid., p. 154.

23. Ibid., p. 164.

24. Marvin Shaw, *The Paradox of Intention: Reaching the Goal by Giving Up the Attempt to Reach It* (Atlanta: Scholars Press, 1988), p. 6.

25. Mary Field Belenky, Blythe McVicker Clinchy, Nancy Rule Goldberger, and Jill Mattuck Tarule, *Women's Ways of Knowing,* p. 3.

Chapter 4

1. Reprinted with permission, anonymously, at author's request.

2. The synopsis included in this chapter comes from my experience in clinical supervision and from my own reflection and experience in clinical practice.

3. The Minnesota model of treatment was revolutionized by the advent of theoretical writing about shame and guilt. Writers such as Gershen Kaufman, Marilyn Mason and Merle Fossum, and John Bradshaw made significant contributions to our understanding of the dynamics of shame, and this theoretical framework provided a critical addition and correction to treatment strategies that had begun to shift toward more punishing models. Kaufman's book, *Shame: The Power of Caring* was the first of many texts on the dynamics of shame. Also noteworthy are Robert Albers, *Shame: A Faith Perspective* (Binghamton, NY: The Haworth Pastoral Press, 1995); John Bradshaw, *Healing the Shame That Binds You* (Deerfield Beach, FL: Health Communications Inc., 1988); Merle Fossum and Marilyn Mason, *Facing Shame: Families in Recovery* (New York: Norton, 1986).

4. Reinhold Niebuhr, *The Nature and Destiny of Man; A Christian Interpretation* (New York: Charles Scribner's Sons, 1948), p. 11.

5. Gershen Kaufman, *Shame: The Power of Caring* (Cambridge: Shenkman Press, 1980), pp. 131-132.

6. Ibid., p. 132.

7. Maya Angelou, *I Know Why the Caged Bird Sings* (New York: Random House, 1969), p. 281.

Chapter 5

1. See James L. Griffith and Melissa Elliott Griffith, *Encountering the Sacred in Psychotherapy: How to Talk with People About Their Spiritual Lives* (New York: Guilford Press, 2002), pp. 24-26; Robert Goodman, Myth and symbols as expressions of the religious, in *Exploring Sacred Landscapes: Religious and Spiritual Dimensions in Psychotherapy,* Mary Lou Randour, Ed. (New York: Columbia University Press, 1993), pp. 113-135.

2. David Tracy, *Blessed Rage for Order: The New Pluralism in Theology* (New York: Seabury Press, 1975), pp. 71, 105. See also Bernard Lonergan, *Method in Theology* (Toronto: University of Toronto Press, 1971); Richard Rohr, *Everything Belongs: The Gift of Contemplative Prayer* (New York: Crossroad Publishing Co., 1999).

3. William James, *The Varieties of Religious Experience; A Study in Human Nature; Being the Gifford Lectures on Natural Religion Delivered at Edinburgh in 1901-1902* (New York: Modern Library, 1902), p. 414.

4. Richard Rohr, Liminal space: Days without answers in a narrow space. *National Catholic Reporter,* February 1, 2002 <natcath.com>, p. 3.

5. Ibid.

6. Ibid., p. 4.

Chapter 6

1. See Mary Field Belenky, Blythe McVicker Clinchy, Nancy Rule Goldberger, and Jill Mattuck Tarule, *Women's Ways of Knowing* (New York: Basic Books, Inc., 1986); Carol Gilligan, *In a Different Voice* (MA: Harvard University Press, 1982).

2. Christie Cozad Neuger, *Counseling Women: A Narrative, Pastoral Approach* (Minneapolis: Augsburg Fortress Press, 2001), pp. 6, 7; 88-90.

3. Ibid., p. 168.

4. Elizabeth Johnson, *She Who Is: The Mystery of God in Feminist Theological Discourse* (New York: Crossroad Publishing Co., 1992), pp. 64, 65.

5. Ibid.

6. Roman Catholic women may find some common ground in this discussion related to their own struggles to continue to say "yes" to the Roman Catholic Church while saying "no" to current formulations of the charism of ministry. A fuller discussion of these ideas can be found in Jeanne McPhee, "Godly Rage: Feminism and Faith in the Roman Catholic Church" (DMin thesis, United Theological Seminary of the Twin Cities, 1995).

7. Mary Farrell Bednarowski, *The Religious Imagination of American Women* (Bloomington: Indiana University Press, 1999), pp. 16-43.

8. Mary Farrell Bednarowski, *The Religious Imagination of American Women,* p. 33.

9. Ibid., p. 42.

10. Sharon Welch, *A Feminist Ethic of Risk* (Minneapolis: Fortress Press, 1990), p. 20.

11. Ibid., pp. 68, 75.

12. Ibid.

13. Stephanie Brown, *Treating the Alcoholic: A Developmental Model of Recovery* (New York: John Wiley & Sons, 1985), p. 15.

14. Cited in Bradley P. Holt, *Thirsty for God: A Brief History of Christian Spirituality* (Minneapolis: Augsburg Fortress Press, 1993).

15. AA Services, *Alcoholics Anonymous; The Story of How Many Thousands of Men and Women Have Recovered from Alcoholism,* Fourth Edition (New York, Alcoholics Anonymous World Services Inc., 1955), pp. 83, 84.

16. Mary Farrell Bednarowski, *The Religious Imagination of American Women,* p. 42.

Chapter 7

1. Elizabeth Johnson, *She Who Is: The Mystery of God in Feminist Theological Discourse* (New York: Crossroad Publishing Co., 1992), p. vii.

2. Ibid.

3. Ibid., p. 250.

Chapter 8

1. George S. Worgul, *From Magic to Metaphor: A Validation of the Christian Sacraments* (New York: Paulist Press, 1980), p. 123.

2. Richard McBrien, *Catholicism,* New Edition, (San Francisco: Harper San Francisco, 1994), p. 9.

3. Ibid., p. 10.

4. Ibid.

5. George S. Worgul, *From Magic to Metaphor,* p. 15.

6. Roberta Bondi, *Memories of God: Theological Reflections on a Life* (Nashville: Abingdon Press. 1995), p. 201. Used by permission.

7. AA Services, *Alcoholics Anonymous; The Story of How Many Thousands of Men and Women Have Recovered from Alcoholism,* Fourth Edition (New York, Alcoholics Anonymous World Services Inc., 1955), p. 84.

8. C.S. Song, *Tell Us Our Names: Story Theology from an Asian Perspective* (Maryknoll, NY: Orbis Books, 1984) p. 37.

9. Huston Smith, *The World's Religions* (San Francisco: Harper Collins Publishers, 1991), p. 387.

10. Ibid.

11. AA Services, *Alcoholics Anonymous,* p. 84.

12. Maureen Sagot, "The Experience of Recovery from Alcoholism: A Perspective of Long-Term Recovered Women." (PhD dissertation, The Union Institute, 1998), p. 8.

Chapter 9

1. Linda Vogel, *Teaching and Learning in Communities of Faith: Empowering Adults Through Religious Education* (San Francisco: Jossey-Bass Publishers, 1991), p. 7.

2. Ibid.

3. Ibid.
4. Ibid.
5. Robert H. Albers, *Shame: A Faith Perspective* (Binghamton, NY: The Haworth Pastoral Press, 1995), p. 138.
6. Ibid., p. 131.
7. Ibid., p. 132
8. C. S. Song, *Tell Us Our Names: Story Tehology from an Asian Perspective* (Maryknoll, NY: Orbis Books, 1984), p. 37.
9. Richard Rohr, Liminal space: Giving up control in life's second half, *National Catholic Reporter,* February 8, 2002 <natcath.com>.
10. Rebecca Chopp, *Saving Work: Feminist Practices in Theological Education* (Louisville, KY: Westminster John Knox Press, 1995), pp. 73-74.
11. Marvin Shaw, *The Paradox of Intention: Reaching the Goal by Giving Up the Attempt to Reach It* (Atlanta: Scholars Press, 1988), p. 202.
12. Richard Rohr, Liminal Space: Giving Up Control in Life's Second Half, *National Catholic Reporter,* February 8, 2002, p. 3.

Chapter 10

1. AA Services, *Alcoholics Anonymous; The Story of How Many Thousands of Men and Women Have Recovered from Alcoholism* (New York: Alcoholics Anonymous Pub., 1955), p. 58.
2. See also Anne Wilson Schaef *Co-Dependence: Misunderstood—Mistreated,* (San Francisco: Harper, 1992).
3. Richard Rohr, Liminal Space: Days without answers in a narrow space. *National Catholic Reporter,* February 1, 2002 <natcath.com>. See also Mircea Eliade, *The Sacred and the Profane: The Nature of Religion,* translated from the French by Willard R. Trask, (San Diego: Harcourt Brace Jovanovich, 1987), *The Myth of the Eternal Return,* translated from the French by Willard R. Trask (Princeton: Princeton University Press, 1974), and William James, *Varieties of Religious Experience* (New York: New American Library, 1958).
4. See Eric J. Cassell, *The Nature of Suffering and the Goals of Medicine* (New York: Oxford University Press, 1991).
5. See Mary Field Belenky, Blythe McVicker Clinchy, Nancy Rule Goldberger, and Jill Mattuck Tarule, *Women's Ways of Knowing* (New York: Basic Books, Inc., 1986); Carol Gilligan, *In a Different Voice* (Cambridge, MA: Harvard University Press, 1982); Stephanie Brown, *Treating the Alcoholic: A Developmental Model of Recovery* (New York: John Wiley & Sons, 1985).
6. AA Services, *Alcoholics Anonymous,* p. 82.
7. C. S. Lewis, *Mere Christianity* (San Francisco: Harper, 1992).
8. AA Services, *Alcoholics Anonymous,* p. 59.

Index

AA
  Big Book, 7, 12, 64-65
  laughter at, 75
  self-description, 7
  story in, 11-12
  twelve traditions, 108
  twelve-step recovery, 7, 92, 93, 107
Abbott Northwestern Chemical
      Dependency Treatment
      Unit, 51
Abuse, shame and, 41-42, 57-58
"Act as if," recovery and, 63-65
Adulterous woman, story of, 86-88
AG (storyteller), God's healing
      presence, 73
Alcoholics Anonymous. See AA
Alcoholics Anonymous, 7
Alcoholism. See also Storytelling
  Columbia, AA members in, 19
  family, author's story, 4
  onset of, MB's story, 13-14, 27-31
  recovery, MH's story, 16-17
  sobriety, MB's story, 36
  what happened, NH's story, 15-16
AM (storyteller), travels in sobriety, 19
"Ambivalence as virtue," 62
Angelou, Maya, 45
Autobiography, spiritual, 93-94
  companions in the journey, 99-100
  conditions at present, 93-94
  continuity, 98-99
  helpers, 102-103
  lessons, 103-104
  life journey, walking and praying,
      97-104
  lifescape, 95-96

Autobiography, spiritual (continued)
  limit experiences, 95
  new life, 104-105
  obstacles, 101-102
  pivotal moments, 97-98
  soulscape, 96-97
  walking the labyrinth, 94

Bednarksi, Mary Farrell, 61
Behavior, while drunk, 28, 29-31,
      86-87
Big Book, AA, 7, 12, 64-65
Bondi, Roberta, 78
Borrowing, shame healed with, 42
Brown, Stephanie, 28, 31, 58, 59, 64

Catastrophic shame, 40-41
Child abuse/abandonment, story, 16-17
Chopp, Rebecca, 7
Companions, life journey, 99-100
Conditions at present, spiritual
      autobiography, 93-94
Confrontation, women by women, 60
  stories of, 15-16, 33
Continuity, life journey, 98-99
Control
  loss of, 29
  temptation to, 64
Conversion, recovery and, 59
Counseling Women: A Narrative,
      Pastoral Approach, 58
Crucifixion experiences, alcoholics,
      71-72

Rising from the Dead
© 2007 by The Haworth Press, Inc. All rights reserved.
doi:10.1300/5800_13